*Putting the
Jewish People
Back at the
Center of
God's Plan*

# Israel
# Matters

JACOB FRONCZAK

# Israel
# Matters

*Putting the Jewish People
Back at the Center of God's Plan*

JACOB FRONCZAK

**Printed in the United States of America**

ISBN: 978-1-892124-98-2

Quantity discounts are available on bulk purchases of this book for educational, fundraising, or event purposes. Special versions or book excerpts to fit specific needs are available from First Fruits of Zion. For more information, contact www.ffoz.org/contact.

## First Fruits of Zion

PO Box 649, Marshfield, Missouri 65706–0649 USA
Phone (417) 468–2741, www.ffoz.org

Comments and questions: www.ffoz.org/contact

*For Reuben*

# Contents

# Introduction

I'm the lead pastor of a nondenominational Christian church. I'm also a Messianic Gentile.

That's a term you might never have heard before. But it means a lot to me. It represents a journey I've taken—not away from Jesus, and not out of the church, but toward something I have found to be beautiful, authentic, and biblical: the realization that Jesus was a Jewish rabbi named Yeshua of Nazareth, that he lived a Jewish life and practiced Judaism, and that when he returns to reign over the earth, he will still be that same faithful practicing Jew.

When this realization hit me, Jesus—Rabbi Yeshua—became more to me than a theological idea. He became more than a checklist of doctrines to be believed. For the first time, I saw Jesus as a real flesh-and-blood person. And with this renewed picture of Jesus in mind, I began to understand the Gospels and the rest of the New Testament—and for that matter, the Old Testament—like I never had before.

I didn't abandon theology; I still believe that Jesus is the Son of God, the Messiah, the Eternal One in whom all the fullness of deity dwells in bodily form, and who is the Word who became flesh and dwelt among us, and whose glory we beheld, the glory of the uniquely begotten Son of God, full of grace and truth.

In my theological framework, Jesus is still Prophet, Priest, and King; in my life, he is still Redeemer, Savior, Friend; but now, on top of that, he is Rabbi. Teacher. King of the Jews.

The preexistent Word, the eternal Son, still finds his place in my doctrinal statement, but the Rabbi from Nazareth is someone I can actually relate to—someone I can connect with, someone I can follow. Someone I, with God's help, can eventually be like.

For me, that's what it means to be a Messianic Gentile. I am a non-Jew following a Jewish rabbi, the Messiah King of Israel. It's hard to explain, but my faith is more *real* than it ever was before. So I hope you can understand why I fully embrace the term "Messianic Gentile" and the journey it represents.

I told the story of that journey in a book called *Yeshua Matters*, because I believe that the broader Christian community desperately needs to see Jesus in his Jewish context. I believe that when Jesus' followers place the risen Rabbi at the center of their faith, wonderful things happen. I believe this because I have seen it in my own life and in the lives of other Christians, and because my theology tells me that the historical person of Jesus the Messiah is the only hope any of us have.

I believe that God has called his church to a better and deeper understanding of his Son and of his Scriptures, and I want to see my brothers and sisters in faith embrace that understanding. I am not asking people to renounce their Christology—I want us to remain believers in the eternal Son of God. But I also want us to discover the joy of following a Jewish rabbi named Yeshua.

On that note, if you don't believe that Jesus was a practicing Jew, or that his disciples remained practicing Jews, or that the very early church saw itself as a sect of Judaism; or if you haven't read the first book in this series, *Yeshua Matters*; I'm afraid you may find this book a little bit confrontational. It wasn't written to be confrontational—not at all. But as we move through the rest of this book together, I am going to take for granted that you are reading this book series in order.

At the risk of tipping my hand, let me explain a bit further. Based on the historical fact that Jesus was a Jewish rabbi, on the following pages I am going to intentionally raise some very difficult questions—questions I struggled with for years without getting any clear answers. From hundreds of conversations I've had over the years, I know I'm not the only Christian who has struggled with these questions.

I spent several years as a youth pastor. During that time, I discovered that Christian teens and young adults are *especially* unsatisfied with some of the traditional answers we've been giving them. They just aren't buying what we're selling—and not because they don't read the Bible or because they don't understand theology. Quite the opposite. When these kids begin to read the Bible for themselves, what they see just doesn't match up with what we're telling them about God.

I am convinced that the Jewish Jesus is the key to answering these questions. With the risen Rabbi as our cornerstone, we can give these kids a solid foundation. But first we have to be willing to talk—we have to start a conversation. We have to acknowledge that we might not be right about everything. We have to ask some hard questions. In my case, I eventually had to question some of my most deeply held assumptions about God, theology, and the Bible. This was a difficult and painful process for me, so I don't expect it to be easy for anyone else.

In fact, through watching others raise some of these same questions, I've learned a few things. I've learned that it's easier to dismiss a question than to answer it. And I've learned that it's easier to attack a person than to attack a problem. I'm sure you've seen this happen—someone with doubts or questions comes to the table to talk, and their questions are ignored. Instead of starting a conversation, those already at the table silence the questioner through a grueling process of character assassination.

I have seen well-meaning Christians refuse to discuss difficult issues, preferring instead to take the low road, to undermine the credibility of anyone who dared to disagree with them. I have watched in horror as Christian leaders I once respected stooped to dirty politics by attacking the orthodoxy, the sincerity, and even the final destiny of anyone who dares to rock their theological boat.

I understand where these Christians are coming from. I understand them because in years past, before I realized that my Rabbi was holding me to a higher standard, I used to do the same thing. I shut people down because I didn't want to answer their questions. And it's not okay; it's never okay to do that. But here's what I know from experience: when we shut people down like that, we do it because we're afraid. We're afraid we might not be right after all. We're afraid that if we go down the rabbit hole, we'll end up in Theology Wonderland, and nothing will make sense anymore, and we won't know what to believe.

I don't want to bring that fear into your life. Fear will turn our conversation into an argument. So before I raise these questions, before I rock the boat, I want to make a few definitive statements.

These statements will guide our discussion; they will serve as our anchor, holding us to theological bedrock so we can feel free to explore the ocean of God's revelation.

First, I and the rest of the First Fruits of Zion staff strongly believe that the Jewish people need the Messiah, Jesus. We believe that Israel's redemption will not be complete until she recognizes the risen Rabbi, Yeshua of Nazareth, as her rightful King. Second, we believe that the Jewish people—not down to the last person, but corporately, as a group—have missed not only the person of Jesus but the prophetic message he delivered to them, and that the Jewish people have a heavenly mandate to obey this message and enthrone Jesus as their Messiah; until this mandate is obeyed, Israel's salvation will be delayed. Finally, we believe that no one, Jew or Gentile, will inherit eternal life apart from the atoning work of Jesus Christ.

I hope that as we continue, you'll be able to keep these statements in mind. While I might question some widely held interpretations of certain Biblical passages, I certainly didn't write this book to put out the fire that Jesus started. Far from it—I have dedicated my life to fanning the flame. But once we understand that our picture of Jesus wasn't as accurate as we thought it was, we have to be willing to go through a process of questioning and reconstructing some of our assumptions. At the end of this tunnel, our vision of Jesus and his relationship with the people of Israel should cause us to rejoice more than ever in the mercy and patience of the God of Abraham. But the tunnel is dark, and while we're inside it, we may not find it easy to remember the promise of light and clarity at its end.

Again, the message of this book supports First Fruits of Zion's mission to reveal Jesus, the Jewish Messiah, to the Jewish people. I hope I demonstrated in *Yeshua Matters* that restoring Jesus' reputation among his people is a key part of this mission. In this book I will try to prove that reevaluating Israel's place in our theology is an important part of restoring Jesus' reputation.

So even as we question some of the theological assumptions that define our relationship with the Jewish people, and even as we push for a more positive, fruitful, and biblical stance in this area, please remember that we are not seeking to uplift Israel at Jesus' expense. Instead, by uplifting Israel, we uplift the Messiah, the gospel of the kingdom, and even the church itself—but first these ideas must be defined and understood in a way that is faithful to what the Bible teaches.

At any rate, if we are on the same page, read on. If not, you may want to save this book for another day.

Finally, before we move on to the topic at hand, I must thank everyone who helped me with the arduous task of writing this book. First and foremost, I give credit to Boaz Michael, whose book *Tent of David* inspired this entire series. In addition, all of the editors and proofreaders, the rest of the FFOZ creative team, and each person who took the time to give me their feedback on early copies—thank you so much for your time and effort. I must especially thank Rabbi Dr. Mark Kinzer, whose kind, lucid, and perceptive feedback changed the shape of this book considerably for the better. May he and everyone else on whom I depended in writing this book have an eternal share in whatever good it might do in the lives of those who read it.

# *Questions*

Ultimately, I believe Yeshua *matters*; it matters that Jesus was Jewish. Knowing that Jesus was Jewish helps us to understand him better than we ever could otherwise. But I've learned that this realization brings a few other issues to the table, questions I never considered in quite the right light before I met the Jewish Jesus. One of those questions concerns Israel.

I don't mean just the land of Israel, although the land matters too. After all, Israel is special. Israel is where the Bible happened. It's where David and Solomon reigned, where Joshua fought the battle of Jericho, where the real presence of God dwelt in the Holy Temple, and where Jesus spent his entire adult life.

Israel has also been in the headlines quite a bit in the last seventy years or so, ever since it was reestablished as a national homeland for the Jewish people—the first Jewish state since before the time of Jesus, and one of the few places in the entire world where a Jewish person can live in safety. Even then, "safety" is a relative term.

At this very moment, as I write, I have my web browser open, and my news feed is full of sound bites and articles about the latest conflict in the Gaza Strip. Everyone has an angle on this conflict. Everyone feels like they need to have an opinion. And not just about recent events in the Middle East. Israel's very *existence* is polarizing. People fight about Israel every day, around the clock and around the world—not just the kind of fighting we see on blogs and social media, but real-life fighting, with fists and guns and bombs. All to answer the question: Do the Jewish people really have a God-given right to live peacefully in their ancient homeland? And what about non-Jewish Palestinians? What about the Arab peoples who inhabited the land of Israel before the establishment of the State of Israel in 1948? Don't they have the right to establish their own nation in Palestine—the right to national self-determination?

But the *real* question lies a little bit deeper than this. It's a question that follows naturally from the idea that Jesus was Jewish. If we believe that Jesus' Jewishness is significant, then we must believe that Jewishness in general is significant—that it means something to be Jewish. We must believe that, biblically speaking, a Jewish person isn't the same as a non-Jewish person.

This leads us to ask a deceptively simple question: "Why?" Why—for what reason and for what purpose—did God choose the Jewish people?

Why were they given what we now call the "Holy Land"? And why do they feature as the major players in the Bible from Genesis chapter 12 through the end of Revelation? And as pretty much the *only* players, the only people of God that we know of, until Acts chapter 10?

And what about today? Does God still have his eye on the Jewish people? On the land of Israel? And if so, what does that mean for everyone else? Does God's relationship with Israel impact Christian theology? If it does, then how?

What changes—if anything—when we put Israel back into the picture?

What do we *do*, theologically speaking, with the Jewish people?

# Boundaries

For years these questions rolled around in the back of my mind. From time to time they would pop up in different forms and I'd wrestle with them again for a while before giving up in frustration. Finally the whole issue boiled down, for me at least, to one critical question: when were the apostles saved?

Let me explain how I got to that question. In *Yeshua Matters* we painted a very Jewish picture of Jesus. He is a Jewish rabbi who practiced Judaism and taught the Jewish way of life to his disciples. But if Jesus' disciples remained practicing Jews, and didn't think they were converting to another religion when they began following Jesus, then when were they "saved"? When and how was their eternal destiny decided? When—and *why*—were their names written in the Book of Life?

If you're an evangelical Christian, you probably believe that the only way to receive eternal life is through believing in Jesus. In other words, Christians are the only people who are "saved." But then what happened to everyone who lived before Jesus came? Were Jesus' disciples "unsaved" until they met him?

Was the Apostle Andrew on his way to eternal hellfire until the day he stopped following John the Baptist, an anointed prophet from God, in order to follow Jesus?[1]

This might seem like a silly question with an obvious answer. But when we break it down, it's not so simple at all. Whether we answer "yes" or "no," we raise a host of new questions, and none of them are easy to answer.

Let's forget about Andrew for a second and zoom out a little bit. Speaking as an evangelical Christian, if we claim to have a sort of monopoly on eternal life (through Jesus), I think an important part of our theology of personal salvation has to do with the question of what happened to all the people who lived and died before Jesus revealed himself to the world. To answer that question, we have to figure out how and when "believing in Jesus" became the way to receive the gift of eternal life.

Believing in Jesus couldn't have been the way Abraham, David, and the other Old Testament saints received that gift. God's couldn't have required people to believe in Jesus before Jesus was born. That wouldn't make any sense. But we know that when Jesus returns, and we sit down together at the great big heavenly banquet table, Abraham, Isaac, and Jacob will be sitting there with us (Matthew 8:11).

If these great Bible heroes didn't "believe in Jesus," then *why are they going to live forever*? On what basis will God forgive their sins and save their eternal souls?

Hopefully by this point you're thinking this problem should be an easy one to solve. All we have to do is look to the Old Testament to find out who received the gift of eternal life before Jesus came. God spent thousands of years revealing himself to the people of Israel through thirty-nine books of law, history, prophecy, wisdom, and song. Surely somewhere in that huge body of literature we should be able to find an answer to this question.

But as soon as we open to the Gospel of Matthew and begin to flip the pages back toward Genesis, we run into a huge problem: the Old Testament doesn't offer any kind of clear answer to the question of personal eternal destiny—or, as we might put it, the question of heaven and hell and who goes where. Of course, we find words we recognize—words like forgiveness, salvation, and redemption—on every page, but there are two important differences between the way these words are used in the Old Testament and the way we are used to using them.

First, these concepts are hardly ever applied to individual people. Instead, we find that God's promises of salvation and redemption were made to an entire nation—the nation of Israel.[2] Second, these words are not really employed to ask or answer the question of what happens to people after they die. As we learned in *Yeshua Matters*, redemption in the Old Testament is almost always described as God's promise to end the exile of the Jewish people, and to place them back into their land where they will dwell in peace and safety forever. When God promised to save the Jewish people, he was promising to save them from the surrounding nations, which threatened again and again to overrun and destroy them.

We do find many passages in the prophets about a coming world full of blessing and peace, but when we look closely at these prophecies, we don't find anything about people going to heaven when they die. Instead, the prophets described this beautiful and picturesque future in terms of the restoration of the whole planet. The words of the prophets are frightfully ambiguous when it comes to the final destinies of all those billions of people who are going to die before that perfect future becomes a reality.

The more time we spend in the Old Testament, the more obvious it becomes that the story we are reading is the story of God's *people* in the singular sense of the word—that is, one people, one corporate unit—and that this people is defined as the nation of Israel.

It may be difficult for you to follow this shift in perspective from an *individual* relationship with God to a *group* relationship with God. Evangelicals, almost by definition, believe that eternal life is given exclusively through a personal relationship with Jesus Christ. God doesn't grant eternal life on the basis of group affiliation or membership; instead, membership in God's people, the church, is granted on the basis of personal salvation. So when we shift our focus from individuals to groups, we are faced with even more questions.

When Jesus died, did God stop dealing with people on a corporate basis and start dealing with people on an individual basis? If not, then did the Jewish people cease to be the people of God at some point? Did they lose the promises of corporate salvation and redemption? Were these promises taken from them and given to another group?

And what about final destinies? Had individual Jewish people ever been promised eternal life because of their membership in God's covenant people? Or had God's promises to and covenants with the nation of Israel never included the final salvation of individual Jews from sin and death? Was God concerned with the final destinies of individuals in the Old Testament era? If he was, why didn't he talk about it? Why don't we find this topic covered in the Law or the Prophets? Until Jesus came, did God's people just have no idea what happened to them after they died? Did they even care? Doesn't everyone care?

And what if God's covenants with the Jewish people *did* include the gift of eternal life to individual Jews? When Jesus died on the cross and rose again, was that gift taken away from every Jewish person who didn't become a Christian? Was Jesus' atoning death *bad news* for most Jewish people?

How did God deal with all those otherwise faithful Jews who fell through the cracks, didn't hear the gospel for one reason or another, or simply didn't understand enough about Jesus to respond to him?

Are they held accountable as individuals for their failure to respond to a message they never heard? Or will God have mercy on them because they are part of a people, Israel, which has had a covenant relationship with God since the days of Abraham?

In short, if some kind of baton was passed from Jews to followers of Jesus, when and how did that happen? How did God's salvation economy shift from Judaism to Christianity? And how did this shift affect the final destinies of individual Jews?

## Promises

This is not an instance of the uncontacted peoples problem, the classic question of the isolated tribesman in a distant land, beyond the reach of the church's missionary efforts. Is it possible for someone to participate in the blessings of eternal life if they never have the opportunity to hear about Jesus? Evangelical Protestant theology has an answer to this question, as unsatisfying as it might be: our poor tribesman is going to hell. You can build that case from a certain interpretation of the Epistle to the Romans and the Gospel of John, but even though I think we might be missing the bigger picture here, this question will have to wait.

Nor is this a question of whether the Jewish people have some end-time significance, some role to play in the coming apocalypse. For over a century, dispensationalists have believed and taught that the Jewish people have a pivotal role in the fulfillment of end-time prophecy. But dispensationalists still take for granted that the nation of Israel has no gracious covenant standing before God. In other words, God has never made any promises that would impact the final destiny of individual Jews *just because they are Jews*. In dispensationalist theology, Jewish people can receive the gift of eternal life only through becoming Christians—through believing in Jesus.

This is not even a question of what happened to that small group of Jews who saw Jesus in the flesh, understood what he was trying to do, and rejected him. That uneasy alliance of corrupt Sadducees, shortsighted Herodians, and hypocritical Pharisees paid dearly in the First Jewish War. Just as Jesus prophesied, the political power bloc that had him crucified was totally destroyed just 40 years after his death and resurrection.

No, this is a different question. It is the question of how a group of people, the Jewish people, can at one moment be unquestionably the people of God, and then in the next moment find themselves outside God's family. Not only that, but the reason the Jewish people have supposedly been disenfranchised—their corporate rejection of Jesus—was, in reality, a situation caused by shortsighted ambition on the part of a very small number of individual Jews.

How could God reverse two thousand years of Jewish history, from Abraham to Jesus, and still claim to be a God who keeps his promises?

How could God permanently end his relationship with the nation he called out of Egypt?

How could God toss aside his covenant people?

This is a difficult question, a heavy question, and whoever would dismiss it out of hand doesn't understand what is at stake.

Imagine a Jewish man praying in a synagogue in the year 26 CE, before Jesus publicly revealed himself. The man prays, full of contrition and repentance: "Have mercy on me, O God, according to your steadfast love; according to your abundant mercy blot out my transgressions. Wash me thoroughly from my iniquity, and cleanse me from my sin" (Psalm 51:1–2). As a Jew, this man is a member of a group that, up to this time, has been God's covenant people for two thousand years. God's promises and covenants with the Jewish people are woven throughout this man's entire Bible (the Old Testament). Knowing this, we ask: Was his prayer heard? Are his sins forgiven?

What about eight years later, in 34 CE, after Jesus' death and resurrection? Let's assume that, through no fault of his own, this man hasn't heard of Jesus. If this pious Jew prays the same prayer with the same heart attitude, and if he is still a member of that same covenant people, is he now rejected? Will he die in his sins? Will he be punished forever?

To believe that God would reject this second prayer is to stretch our faith, our compassion, and our common sense beyond their limits. If we believe that God never heard his prayers to begin with, we make nonsense of the entire Old Testament—why would God inspire David to write a book of psalms for the Jewish nation, then close his ears to the prayers of that people? But if we believe that God heard and accepted this pious Jew's second prayer, we throw a wrench into our theology. How can his sins be forgiven if he hasn't accepted Jesus as his Lord and Savior?

This example illustrates a larger point. If we believe that God passed over the Jewish people in favor of Christians, corporately replacing one people with another, then we are forced to reinterpret or ignore chapter upon chapter of the Old Testament, each one full of prophecies and promises that point to the restoration of the Jewish people in a permanent state of covenant blessing and peace (as we will show in a later chapter).

Our example of the pious Jew who missed the Jesus memo also raises another, even more unsettling question: could God turn around and reject Christians as well? If he can break his promises to one people, why not another? After all, some of God's covenants with the Jewish people are unilateral and unconditional; they are simply promises. These promises do not depend on the Jewish people at all—not on their obedience, and not on their faithfulness, but on God's faithfulness (try Jeremiah 31:37 on for size). If God can break those promises, couldn't he break the ones he made to us? Could we one day find ourselves condemned because we didn't listen to some new prophet?

On the other hand, if we believe that God has *not* passed over the Jewish people, if we believe that they still inherit God's gracious promises to Abraham, then we pierce the heart of evangelical *ecclesiology*—our theology of the church, our answer to the question of who belongs in God's family.

We are even more disturbed when we realize that if God continued to hear the prayers of pious Jews who never heard about Jesus, then the eternal destiny of individual Jews may follow from Israel's covenant relationship with God, instead of hinging on their personal acceptance of Jesus as the Messiah. If we believe that Jewish people can be saved without hearing about, knowing about, or believing in Jesus, we pierce the heart of evangelical *soteriology*, our theology of personal salvation—what it is, how it happens, and who it happens to.

So which is it? Either (1) the Jewish people continue to enjoy a covenant relationship with God based on gracious and unconditional promises, and this covenant may bring eternal life to individual Jews; or (2) the Jewish people used to have this kind of covenant relationship with God, but they don't anymore, or (3) the Jewish people never had this kind of covenant relationship with God. One of these three options, or a slight variation of one of these options, must be true. It will do no good to skirt around the issue. We will eventually find ourselves on one side or another. We will categorically condemn non-Jesus-believing Jewish people as isolated from God, strangers to his grace, and condemned to hell, or we will revise our answer to the questions, "who are the people of God?" and, "how does someone inherit eternal life?"

My hope is that by the end of this book the choice will be clear.

*Part 1*

# Definitions

As soon as we begin talking about Jews, Gentiles, Israel, and the church, we run into difficult territory. Who is Jewish, and who is not? What does it mean to be a Gentile? What is the church? And who is Israel? You may be surprised at some of the answers that have been offered in response to these questions—and why it is so important to get these answers right.

As we go through these four categories, it will be important to remember that we are primarily discussing groups, and not individuals. As we will see, God sometimes deals with individuals, but in the grand scope of the biblical narrative, God often deals with entire groups all at once—that is, corporately. He makes categorical statements about these groups and establishes corporate relationships with them.

This doesn't mean that individuals experience God only through membership in a group. Sometimes God chooses to deal with individuals regardless of which group they are in. Other times, though, righteous people in a group that is cursed will suffer along with their group. The converse is true as well; evil people in a group that is blessed often enjoy God's provision along with their group. But these exceptions shouldn't blind us to the fact that God still deals with groups, and not only with individuals.

# The Jewish People

*They are Israelites, and to them belong the
adoption, the glory, the covenants, the giving of
the law, the worship, and the promises. To them
belong the patriarchs, and from their race,
according to the flesh, is the Christ, who is God
over all, blessed forever. Amen.*

— Romans 9:4–5

Who is a Jew? I mean, how do you define Jewishness? Go ahead
and answer—you probably have some idea.

I don't want to go any further until you've answered the question for yourself.

Got it?

All right.

Someone would take offense at your answer. How do I know
this? Because no matter how you answer the question, you exclude
someone who believes they should be included, or you include
someone whom many people believe should be excluded.

If you say, "A Jewish person is someone born to a Jewish mother
or who converts to Judaism under the supervision of an Orthodox
Jewish rabbi," you exclude many Jews who identify as Jewish based
on patrilineal descent—that is, their mother was not Jewish, but
their father was. Many Reform Jews fall into this category.

So who are you to tell someone they're not Jewish?

But if you say, "A Jewish person is someone born to a Jewish father or mother or who converts to Judaism under the supervision of any rabbi who is recognized by his faith community," you include many who would not be considered Jewish by orthodox, or traditional, standards. Some would accuse you of blurring the difference between Jew and Gentile, and ultimately threatening the very definition of Jewish identity.

So who are you to move the goalposts—to redefine Jewishness?

You're going to offend somebody. You lose if you even try to answer the question.

The purpose of this chapter is *not* to take a stand in this very sensitive area—it would be a foolish, lose-lose proposition. I use this issue only as an example to help us understand the problem we will face as we begin to explore these important definitions. As we begin to nail down who is "in" and who is "out"—those who fall into category A and those who fall into category B—and ultimately how these distinctions impact the eternal destinies of human beings, we tread on thin ice.

I didn't write this chapter to offend anyone. I also don't want to give the impression that my opinion is somehow relevant to the Jewish community. It isn't. As a Gentile, I have no standing in that community, and I'm not trying to impose my definitions on it. In any definition of who or what constitutes the Jewish people, I ultimately defer to the Jewish people.

Someone reading this book is thinking—defer to the Jewish people? Why not defer to God?

Great question. Let's tackle it. As we do, we'll get a lesson in Jewish history that few Bible readers take the time to learn—a lesson that will help us make sense of Jesus' and the apostles' statements regarding Jews, Gentiles, and the church.

## Adjudication

If you're a Protestant, you're probably used to a certain paradigm of spiritual authority: God inspired the Bible, individual Christians read the Bible, and those individuals apply what they have read to their life of faith. While pastors and elders may have limited authority within their congregations, Protestants generally don't believe that they are required to agree with everything their pastor says. Every disciple of Jesus has both the right and the responsibility to read and follow the Bible, because the Bible is our final authority, the ultimate source to which we must all look as we seek to develop our beliefs and practices.

If you believe that the gift of prophecy is alive and active today, then you may also believe that God has given some people other messages, other revelations besides the Scripture. But aside from these prophetic messages, Protestants generally believe that there is no truly authoritative teaching outside of what is revealed in the Bible.[3] This belief is referred to as *sola scriptura*, and it lies very close to the heart of what it means to be a Protestant.

Roman Catholics have a very different paradigm of spiritual authority. Of course, Catholics see the Bible as an authoritative source; but Catholicism is also defined by the Magisterium, a body of authoritative teaching that has come from *within the church*. Certain people in the Catholic Church are seen as having the authority to make pronouncements that carry real weight in the life of a Roman Catholic. These constitutions, encyclicals, and other such pronouncements are binding; a devout Catholic can't choose whether or not to accept them. On the other hand, these pronouncements aren't prophetic oracles or inspired Scriptures; they don't claim to be messages directly from God.

Protestants have never accepted the Magisterium; to a Protestant, even the most treasured pronouncements, catechisms, and statements of faith are considered authoritative only to the degree that they are drawn directly from the Scriptures.

Of course, Protestants *do* believe and teach that their statements of faith, creeds, and other expressions of doctrine are drawn directly from the Scriptures. If Protestants didn't think their doctrinal statements were biblical, they wouldn't have them in the first place, because the Protestant's ultimate spiritual authority is the Bible.

But—and I speak as a member of a Protestant church—if our ultimate authority is the Bible, and not the creeds and doctrines of the church, then why do we even have doctrinal statements? And why do all of these statements look a little different, even while all of them claim to be biblical? The answer is that the Bible leaves a few things unsaid. Sometimes it's is very clear, but sometimes it isn't.

So there is actually a step missing in the way I described the Protestant paradigm of spiritual authority at the beginning of this section. In practice, what we really believe looks more like this: God inspired the Scripture; *we read, interpret, and adjudicate the Scripture*; and we apply the principles that we extract to our life of faith.

Interpretation is the process of finding out exactly what a Scripture passage means.

Adjudication is very similar but more specific. It is the process of deciding *whether and how a law or commandment applies in a given situation.*

To use a fictional example: Imagine that we all live in a land in which the laws are very simple. Let's call it Simple Land. One of the laws in Simple Land is "Do not murder." All of us in Simple Land agree that "Do not murder" is a good law.

But what is murder? How is it defined? Is all killing murder? Is it murder to kill someone who has a knife to your throat? Is it murder to kill someone who has threatened to kill you and is on his way to your house with a deadly weapon? Is it murder to kill someone who has killed an innocent person? Is it murder to kill a cow?

These kinds of questions are settled through adjudication. When citizens of Simple Land find themselves in one of the above situations, they are brought before a court, and the court finds them guilty or not guilty. In the process, the definition of murder is clarified—the judges of Simple Land decide that *this* is murder and *that* is not murder. This decision, this clarification, is recorded for future reference. This is called precedent, or case law.

At some point in the future, another citizen of Simple Land might find himself in the same situation. At that point, the judges of Simple Land look back at the precedent, the case law that was set the last time the same thing happened. And they know: this is murder; that is not.

Most of us already know a little bit about case law. You have probably seen or heard references to United States case law, perhaps without even knowing it. For example, almost everyone has heard of the Miranda warning, which police officers are required to read to suspects before interrogation—"You have the right to remain silent," and so forth. This important procedure was clarified in a famous court case: Miranda v. Arizona, 384 U.S. 436 (1966).

The Supreme Court of the United States set an important precedent by throwing out the government's case against Miranda, based on the fact that he had not been made aware of his rights. To help clarify the law and make future cases easier to decide, the Supreme Court judges clearly spelled out what law enforcement officials have to tell their suspects before interrogation. Now everyone can look at the precedent and know: this kind of confession is admissible; that kind is not.

It is important to record case law so that every person who encounters the same situation is judged in the same way, by the same standard. The system would be unjust if the judge got to decide that murder is defined one way for you, but another way for someone else. It would be unjust if some suspects knew about their Miranda rights, but other suspects were kept in the dark.

It so happens that "Do not murder," a simple law for our Simple Land, is also a commandment in the Bible. Most of the laws in the Bible are simple, especially when compared to the laws of modern nations. In fact, sometimes the Bible's laws are so vague that it is nearly impossible to obey them without either making some decisions or making some assumptions. (What does it mean to "remember the Sabbath day, and keep it holy"?)

The Bible's ambiguity in these areas isn't necessarily a bad thing. Simple laws are good. There are so many situations that a human being might encounter that it would be impossible to address every single possibility in specific terms. In this way the Bible is kind of like the United States Constitution: it provides overarching guidance in terms that are often extremely broad. It doesn't attempt to specifically address every single thing that could ever happen.

But if we are supposed to believe that the Bible is the ultimate authoritative source for our walk of faith, then we must also believe that even though the Bible is not always very specific, it *does* speak to every single human situation, no matter how bizarre or unprecedented. If this is the case, then there must be an adjudication process to decide how the Bible applies in new or unique situations—just as with any other law code.[4]

Who gets to adjudicate? Whose job is it to clarify what is murder and what is not? Who decides how the laws and commandments of the Bible apply?

# Delegation

It would be wonderful if God had given us ultra-specific directions for every possible situation. But he hasn't—at least, not in the Bible.

It would also be wonderful if the presence of the Holy Spirit among us caused us to be unified in the way we interpret and adjudicate the Bible's commandments. But if we get two Christians together to try to make sense of a Bible passage, we'll probably get at least three opinions.[5]

If we treat the Bible as a personal discipleship manual that each believer in Jesus gets to interpret on his own, as has become the *de facto* practice in the lives of many evangelical Protestants, we end up with an unjust system—a different standard for everyone. One person might think it is okay to, for example, get a tattoo; someone else might think tattoos are prohibited. But they can't both be right. The Bible has to apply to everyone equally. Even if some category of people is treated differently, that category also has to be clear in the Bible itself. We don't get to give ourselves special exemptions from the law—not the law of the country we live in, and not the law of God.

So we need adjudication. But who gets to do it? Who gets to decide?

In the case of the Old Testament law, the Torah, we have a clear answer:

> If any case arises requiring decision between one kind of homicide and another, one kind of legal right and another, or one kind of assault and another, any case within your towns that is too difficult for you, then you shall arise and go up to the place that the LORD your God will choose. And you shall come to the Levitical priests and to the judge who is in office in those days, and you shall consult them, and they shall declare to you the decision. Then you shall do according to what they declare to you from that place that the LORD will choose. And you shall be careful to do according to all that they direct you. According to the instructions that they give you, and according to the decision which they pronounce to you, you shall do. You shall not turn aside from the verdict that they

declare to you, either to the right hand or to the left. The man who acts presumptuously by not obeying the priest who stands to minister there before the LORD your God, or the judge, that man shall die. So you shall purge the evil from Israel. (Deuteronomy 17:8–12)

This passage is clearly about adjudication. It records a mandate from God, given through Moses, to create an important part of the framework for a civil judicial system in ancient Israel. In this system, the Torah was the law of the land—not a personal manual for living, but a real code of laws for a real nation.

In ancient Israel, when someone broke the Torah, they were brought before a local court. It's just like when someone is arrested and tried for breaking the laws of any modern nation; they go to the courthouse and argue their case (or, more commonly, a lawyer argues for them). When a civil or criminal case was too hard for a local court, the plaintiff and defendant had to argue their case before the highest court in the land, in "the place that the LORD your God will choose" (later on we learn that this place is Jerusalem). This isn't so different from the appeals process in many countries today; in America, for instance, truly unprecedented cases are often argued before the Supreme Court.

According to Deuteronomy 17, the ancient "Supreme Court" of Israel—composed of the judges and the Levitical priests—declared its decision from Jerusalem, and the people who brought their case before the court were required to obey that decision.

But look more closely at the language in this passage. Why would the court have to "declare" its decision? This makes it sound like a public event—a big deal, something everyone was supposed to know about. Then Moses goes on for several sentences about how important it is for the people to obey the decisions of the judges. Knowing that adjudication is a necessary part of any judicial system, it seems safe to assume from Moses' language here that these decisions became part of ancient Israelite "case law." Every time a decision was made, a precedent was set, and from that point on throughout the whole land, the law—the Torah—had to be interpreted according to that decision. After a precedent had been set, when similar cases were brought before lower courts, they could just look back at the precedent and rule in the same way.

It is important to recognize that God *delegated,* or gave away, the responsibility of adjudicating the Old Testament law. Specifically, he gave this responsibility to the Levitical priests and the judges in Jerusalem.

God entrusted the leaders of the Jewish people with the responsibility to adjudicate the laws he gave to them. In fact, because God personally set up the system, and commanded the Jewish people to obey the decisions of the judges, Jewish "case law" had the stamp of God's approval *before any case was ever tried.* He told the people of Israel in advance, "Whatever the priests and judges decide, you must do." In setting up the system this way, God gave up direct control over the specific shape the Law of Moses would take. He let his people take a part of that responsibility. He delegated.[6]

While the idea of Jewish "case law" is similar to the Catholic Magisterium, it really has no Protestant equivalent. In fact, it may be unsettling for someone from a Protestant background to imagine God giving this level of responsibility to humans, to ordinary people who can make mistakes.

But we can't get around the fact that God commanded the Jewish people to obey the decisions of the judges and priests. We must accept that God delegates, and that spiritual authority in this case exists outside the text of the Bible, though it draws its legitimacy directly from the Bible—or, perhaps more accurately, from the event recorded in the Bible, in which God through Moses commanded the Jewish people to defer to the judges and priests.

At the time when Moses spoke the words recorded in Deuteronomy, the people of Israel had been redeemed from slavery. They were free. They were not ruled by any other nation; they were ruled by God alone. After forty years of wilderness wandering, they were finally ready to conquer the land of Canaan. After they took possession of the land, they eventually asked God to give them a king. In time, the Jewish people set up a civil government that ruled over all twelve tribes. This government must have included a civil judicial system something like the court system most countries have today. The judges in this system would have adjudicated the Law of Moses during the time of the ancient kings of Israel based on the directions God gave to Moses in the above-quoted passage.

When Israel was sent into exile in 586 BCE, her civil judicial system was destroyed along with the rest of her civil government.

However, the Jewish people were not relieved of the responsibility of adjudicating the Law of Moses. Instead, according to Jewish tradition, the spiritual leaders of the community of Israel in the time of Ezra reestablished the judicial system. Jewish lore records that the last of the great Old Testament prophets were present at the first meeting of the newly established court in Jerusalem, and that they placed God's blessing on Ezra's rebuilt system. Just as in the time of the ancient kings of Israel, laymen who were experts in the Torah, along with the Levitical priests, would continue to interpret and adjudicate the laws of God for their countrymen.[7]

This governing body was known as the Sanhedrin. In matters of obedience to the Law of Moses, the decisions of the Sanhedrin were authoritative—the Jewish people had to obey them, just as Moses had instructed in Deuteronomy 17. We learn from Acts 23:6 that the Sanhedrin in Jesus' time had members from at least two groups: the Pharisees (primarily laymen who were experts in the Law) and the Sadducees (primarily Levitical priests). So even though the people of Israel were not self-governing in a civil or political sense, as they had been in the time when Moses gave the commandments regarding adjudication, they still had "the Levitical priests" and "the judge who is in office" (Deuteronomy 17:9) to continue to resolve disputes, create precedents, and establish case law. Though Rome governed the Jewish people according to Roman *civil* law, the Sanhedrin had complete authority when it came to issues that were outside the scope of Roman law. For the most part, these issues were confined to Jewish *religious* expression.

Matthew 23:2–3 indicates that Jesus himself recognized the group of men who occupied the "seat of Moses," the Sanhedrin, as the proper adjudicating body of Jewish law. Even as he loudly rebuked these very same leaders when they failed to live up to the standard to which they held everyone else, Jesus commanded his disciples to obey the rulings of the Sanhedrin, just as Moses commanded the ancient Israelites to obey the rulings of the Levitical priests and the judges in Jerusalem.[8]

# Yavneh

A few decades after the ascension of the Master, the First Jewish-Roman War broke out. Untold numbers of Jews were massacred. The Sanhedrin found its traditional meeting place—a room on the Temple Mount in Jerusalem—destroyed by Roman legions, along with the rest of the Temple and most of the city.

But the Jewish people were not relieved of the responsibility of adjudicating the Law of Moses.

Knowing this, a rabbi named Yochanan ben Zakkai reestablished the Sanhedrin at Yavneh, sometimes anglicized as Jamnia.

The Jewish community accepted this new arrangement.[9] As the Temple no longer stood, and the Jewish people had completely lost the ability to govern themselves, we might think that a Sanhedrin—the equivalent of a Supreme Court—could no longer function. How can a nation have a judicial system when it has no civil government?

But in reality, the guidance of a Sanhedrin was needed more than ever. Since the Temple had been destroyed, it was not clear how Israel was supposed to obey many of the laws of the Torah that referenced or depended on the Temple. We also need to remember that the traditional Jewish community never accepted the Christian idea that the Temple was supposed to be destroyed forever, or that animal sacrifices were supposed to be put to an end after Jesus came. The leaders of the Jewish community felt strongly that they needed to preserve the specific rites and procedures involved in Temple worship, so that at some future time the sacrificial system could be reinstated.

A few decades after the Temple was destroyed, another war broke out between Rome and Jerusalem. This time, the results were even more catastrophic. Jerusalem was totally leveled. The Jewish people were banned from their ancient homeland. They were scattered throughout the Empire. As Christianity slowly grew in power and influence, the Jewish people were increasingly singled out for persecution. When the Roman Empire was finally Christianized, this persecution only intensified. One unfortunate result of this persecution was the final dissolution of the Sanhedrin.

But even without a Sanhedrin, without a high court in Jerusalem, without the civil judicial system of ancient Israel, the Jewish people were not relieved of the responsibility of adjudicating the Law of Moses. Traditional Jews believe that the Torah is still valid and in force today, and with any law comes the need for adjudication. So ever since the Sanhedrin was dissolved, the Jewish community has relied on its rabbis to settle disputes, to establish case law, and to decide how the Law of Moses, the Torah, is to be lived out in an ever-changing world.

It may seem like a stretch to connect today's rabbis with the four-thousand-year-old command of God through Moses to set up a judicial system for the Jewish nation. So much has changed in the intervening time. We should also keep in mind that today's rabbis don't hold the same level of authority as a Sanhedrin would; they don't have the authority to *replace* the highest court in the land of Israel (though they may someday *reestablish* it). Rabbis are more limited in what they can adjudicate.

But there will always be a need for clarification, for settling disputes, and for dealing with new circumstances. There is no one outside the Jewish community who can decide how these things are done within the Jewish community. We have no real choice but to accept that the Jewish community must, however it deems appropriate, continue to carry the torch forward and adjudicate the Torah.[10]

## Community

So we come back to the question—who is a Jew?

This is a question that only the Jewish community can answer. It is an issue of adjudication. The Torah specifies that some laws apply to everyone in Israel, while other laws are specifically given only to Jewish people.[11] Because of this distinction in the Torah, the adjudicators of the Jewish community must determine who those laws apply to and who they don't apply to. They must decide who is Jewish and who is not.

Currently, the Jewish community—at least, what an outsider would see as the Jewish community—is divided on this question. In other words, the answer to the question, "who is a Jew?" depends on who you ask.

However, we can safely make some blanket statements that should help us understand who has the right to call himself a Jew and who does not.

Let's start with a question: How do people come to be Jewish? When someone says, "I'm Jewish," how do they know?

There are two answers to this question—two entry points into Jewish identity. The first is by birth; one can be born into a Jewish family in a Jewish community, a community that has taken the time to define and guard its Jewish identity. The second is by conversion; someone who was not born Jewish can convert to Judaism and join a Jewish community later in life.

Knowing this helps us to realize right away that Jewishness is not an easy concept to define—at least, not in our modern world.

As we look back at the Old Testament, we find that the Jewish people were originally called the "children of Israel," or "Israelites." "Israel" was the name God gave to Abraham's grandson Jacob. Israelites are literal, physical children of Israel; that's the plain meaning of the word "Israelite." So we might define the Jewish people as Jacob's descendants.

But while that is probably how the word was first used, let's not forget that from the very beginning of Israel's history, great numbers of people from other nations have joined the Jewish community—they have become Jewish. At the same time, many of Jacob's descendants have left their identity as Jews behind and have assimilated into other people groups. So being Jewish is not about pure bloodlines, perfect genealogies, or forgotten ancestries. In other words, even though most Jews are born Jewish, Jewishness is not *solely* an ethnic designation.

The Torah makes it clear that non-Jews could live in Israel among the Jewish people and were not required to follow all of the same laws a Jewish person had to follow. Using modern terminology, they might be called resident aliens. Similarly, today many non-Jews live in the modern nation of Israel. It is possible to be an Arab Israeli. But unless these immigrants and resident aliens formally adopt the *religion* of Judaism through a process called ritual proselytization, they cannot become Jewish. So Jewishness is not *solely* a national designation either—at least, not in the secular sense of national identity that most of us are used to.

So maybe Jewishness is best understood in religious terms. After all, for thousands of years Jewish people have had a common bond in their religious heritage. One can even become Jewish through a formal conversion process, much like one can convert to any other religion. However, when someone becomes Jewish through ritual proselytization, their religion isn't the only thing that changes. The conversion is deeper than that; it changes the whole identity of the convert. Proselytes don't become Scottish Jews or Indian Jews or Japanese Jews; they just become Jewish. (When a double-identifier like "Spanish Jew" or "German Jew" is used, the first term refers to a shared national, ethnic, and religious background *within* Judaism, and not to the ethnicity of a proselyte before conversion.) Finally, to add one more complication, many Jews have abandoned their religious heritage; they still identify as Jews but do not practice any form of Judaism. So Jewishness is not *solely* a religious designation.

So what is Jewishness? What does it really mean to be Jewish?

Jewishness is best understood as a nationality, but only if we set aside our modern, secular idea of what a nation is. In the ancient world, nationality had ethnic and religious components. These components were not really thought of in separate categories. While today someone can be an ethnic Korean practicing Hinduism as an American citizen, two thousand years ago people didn't have those kinds of choices. (In many nations today people still don't have these kinds of choices—minorities are often persecuted for their religion or ethnicity outside the Western world.)

Ancient nations were not really distinguishable from ethnic groups, and each nation had its own national religion based on the worship of ancient familial gods. The Jewish people have retained this ancient definition of national identity. So even though some Jews are not physically descended from Abraham, all Jews look to Abraham as their patriarch; and even though some Jews do not practice Judaism, Judaism is still the national religion of the Jewish people, and it is rooted in the worship of the God of Abraham, the God of Isaac, the God of Jacob—the God of Israel.

Just like a nation collectively decides who belongs to it, the Jewish community is a self-defining group. Who is defined as Jewish? Whoever meets the standards of the Jewish community. No one can be Jewish without some relationship to the Jewish community. No one can become Jewish without formally adopting the religion of Judaism. And no one can stop being Jewish once they are Jewish, although they *can* decide not to bring their children into the Jewish community.

So neither Jewish ancestry nor Israeli citizenship nor the adoption of the religion of Judaism (apart from formal proselytization) makes one automatically Jewish. In the end, to be Jewish is to be part of the Jewish community on their terms—and no one else's.

## Covenants

At the heart of what it means to be Jewish is the relationship the Jewish people have with God by virtue of the covenants God has made with them.

A covenant is like a contract or a promise. Some covenants are conditional; they have requirements or promises on both sides. In this kind of covenant, everyone involved has to hold up their end of the deal—"I'll scratch your back if you scratch mine." If one side fails to perform, the other side can break their end of the agreement as well.

Other covenants are one-sided; they are simply unconditional promises. I like the term "unilateral" for these kinds of covenants because it's such a powerful word—it reminds us that someone who makes this kind of promise makes it on their own terms, on their own initiative; they make a firm commitment even though they may get nothing out of the deal. In either case, whether conditional or unconditional, a covenant with God is serious business. God never breaks covenant with anyone; he is faithful to do everything he says he will do.

The first covenant between God and the Jewish people was made with the patriarch Abraham. This covenant was originally conditional on Abraham's obedience; God promised a number of things to Abraham, but only if Abraham would do what God commanded. Since Abraham did what God commanded, God is forever bound by his promises to Abraham. This covenant is now unconditional, sealed forever by Abraham's faithful obedience.

This covenant is found in Genesis 12:1–3:

> Now the LORD said to Abram, "Go from your country and
> your kindred and your father's house to the land that I

will show you. And I will make of you a great nation, and I will bless you and make your name great, so that you will be a blessing. I will bless those who bless you, and him who dishonors you I will curse, and in you all the families of the earth shall be blessed."

The very next verse states that Abraham went as God had told him to. He fulfilled his end of the covenant. At that point God had obligated himself to do several things for Abraham. In doing so, he made Abraham a unique person; no one else at that time enjoyed such a personal relationship with the God of creation. To reiterate—this is such an important point—from this point in history onward, God's promises to Abraham became absolutely unconditional. Because Abraham was faithful, God is forever obligated to carry out his side of what is now called the Abrahamic covenant.

In Genesis 17 we find that God expanded on his promise to Abraham. In addition to making Abraham's descendants a great nation and giving them a land to possess, he promised to extend the unique relationship between Abraham and God to Abraham's descendants: "I will establish my covenant between me and you and your offspring after you throughout their generations for an everlasting covenant, to be God to you and to your offspring after you" (Genesis 17:7).

These passages make it clear that God promised to be the national God of Abraham's descendants. However, a stipulation, a sort of condition, was put on this promise. Abraham's descendants would have to hold up their end of the deal in order to be a part of the Abrahamic covenant: "This is my covenant, which you shall keep, between me and you and your offspring after you: Every male among you shall be circumcised" (Genesis 17:10). Anyone who did not follow through with circumcision did not get to remain part of the Jewish people: "Any uncircumcised male who is not circumcised in the flesh of his foreskin shall be cut off from his people; he has broken my covenant" (Genesis 17:14).

We can learn several things from this passage. First, this covenant clearly refers to Abraham's physical descendants—to the nation that God is going to create through Abraham's grandson Israel. As a child, you may have sung, "Father Abraham had many sons … I am one of them, and so are you." In a sense, this is true, as we will see in a later chapter. But when we read this chapter in its historical context, as it was originally understood, we don't see room for anyone outside of the nation of Israel. This specific promise, along with the requirement to be circumcised, is specifically directed toward the physical descendants of Abraham. This is the plain meaning of the passage, and Abraham certainly would have understood God's promise in this way.

Again, you might be thinking—What about me? Even if I'm not Jewish, the Apostle Paul wrote that I'm a child of Abraham by faith—right? Doesn't that mean that God really had *me* in mind, and not the Jewish people, when he made these promises to Abraham?

Bear with me—we will get to these questions shortly. But before we get to the New Testament, we need to make sure we understand the plain, sensible, surface-level meaning of these Old Testament passages. We'll get into more detail on why this is important, but this interpretation of Genesis, because it is properly grounded in its historical context, will give us a solid foundation from which to understand everything that happened afterward.

Moving on, the second thing we learn from this passage is that the Abrahamic covenant, including the command to physically circumcise Abraham's physical descendants, lasts forever. Canaan is said to be the "everlasting possession" of the Jewish people (Genesis 17:8), and the covenant is to last "throughout their generations" (Genesis 17:9); it is an "everlasting covenant" (Genesis 17:13).

Third, anyone born into the nation of Israel who is not circumcised is "cut off from his people" (Genesis 17:14). In a practical sense, that person's children will probably not identify as Jewish and, as such, will probably lose their Jewish identity.

## Circumcision

By the time of Jesus, the term "circumcision" or "circumcised" had become an idiom. Idioms are words or phrases that develop their own meanings; they are not really defined by the words they contain. For example, "burning the midnight oil" is an idiom for staying up late in order to work or study. No oil is necessarily involved; the phrase doesn't refer to actual burning at all. It's an idiom.

"Circumcision" was an idiom in Jesus' time. To be "circumcised" was to be Jewish; to be "uncircumcised" was to be a Gentile.[12] A Gentile could be circumcised in the surgical sense, but he would not be called "circumcised." He would still be called "uncircumcised," because he had not joined the Jewish community through the proper channels (formal proselyte conversion). When a Gentile did choose to undergo proselyte conversion to Judaism, the entire process was called "circumcision," even though there was more to the process than the surgical act.

The reason the word "circumcised" worked so well as an idiom for "Jewish" was because *only* Jewish men were circumcised and *every* Jewish man was circumcised. And even if this wasn't the case (even if other cultures practiced some form of circumcision), it was close enough to being true that the idiom worked, and it stuck. Circumcision in Jesus' time and culture was a clearly defined characteristic of a Jewish man, and this difference between Jews and Gentiles created a social barrier between the groups. Jews and Gentiles were just different, and everyone knew on which side of the divide they fell.

In both the Old and New Testaments, the term "circumcision" has yet another non-literal use; it can refer to a change of heart. Moses told the Israelites, "Circumcise therefore the foreskin of your heart" (Deuteronomy 10:16); Paul wrote, "Circumcision is a matter of the heart" (Romans 2:29).

Some Christians believe Paul is teaching that Jesus did away with circumcision when he came to earth, and that the state of our hearts is all that matters. But the imagery of a circumcised heart was never intended to replace the physical practice of circumcision. Paul is probably referencing Moses, who used the same imagery to illustrate an inward reality that God desires to see in the heart of every Jewish person.

## Identity

God's covenant with Abraham, as it was modified in Genesis 17, created a distinct group of people with a distinct identity and a distinct relationship with God. The covenant was described as perpetual, everlasting, never-ending.

The people with whom God made that covenant were the physical descendants of Abraham. In Genesis 17:21 we read that God narrowed the promise, singling out one of Abraham's eight sons: Isaac. Of Isaac's two sons, only one inherited the promise: Jacob (Genesis 28:13–15; see also 1 Chronicles 16:16–17).

But with Jacob's children, God stopped narrowing his focus. Jacob was given the name "Israel," and the Israelites, the children of Israel, corporately inherited the promises that God gave to Abraham. They were to be circumcised, and as long as they were faithful to maintain that marker of identity as Abraham's children, they were legally entitled to all the blessings of the Abrahamic covenant, including the land of Canaan (today called Israel) and a corporate relationship with God: "I will be their God" (Genesis 17:8).

Of course God is their God; he is the God of everyone and everything. So when he says "I will be *their* God," he promises that they will have a unique relationship with him, a relationship that the other nations of the world do not enjoy.

The Jewish people have carried this covenant identity with them until the present day, and they show every sign of being willing and able to carry it forward indefinitely. The resilience of the Jewish people and of Jewish tradition has even been acknowledged in popular culture. When the New York Times printed a Millennium Edition on January 1, 2000, the editors speculated as to what the front page of the newspaper would look like on January 1, 2100. While most of the headlines were fanciful and outlandish, there was a small advertisement on the front page informing Jewish families of the candle-lighting time for the coming Sabbath evening. This might sound funny, but any humor in the Times' gesture comes from the fact that on January 1, 2100, whatever else may have changed in the world, we can be absolutely certain that traditional Jewish families will still be lighting Sabbath candles.

So God's covenant with Abraham gave the Jewish people a unique identity and a unique relationship with him. But does this covenant, this relationship, include any guarantee of an eternal hope? Do God's promises to the Jewish people speak only to this life, or do they speak to the next as well?

# Destiny

God made many covenants with the Jewish people. However, to address the question of their eternal destiny, one covenant in particular deserves our attention.

At one point in history, the actions of the Jewish people were so abhorrent to God that he empowered the armies of Babylon to conquer their land, allowed the holy Temple to be destroyed, and sent his people into exile. This calamity left a lasting mark on the Jewish people; the idea of exile is still ingrained into the Jewish psyche.

But throughout those dark days God had a message of hope. One of the most outspoken prophets of the exile, and the one who prophesied the destruction of the Temple and the Babylonian conquest in some of the clearest terms, was Jeremiah. In the last part of his book, Jeremiah recorded another prophecy—a prophecy of Israel's future, a prophecy of the destiny of the Jewish people.

This particular oracle begins in Jeremiah 30 and goes through chapter 31. We won't print the entire prophecy here, but you should probably read both chapters on your own. The prophecy is directed toward "my people, Israel and Judah" (Jeremiah 30:3); that is, the physical descendants of Abraham through his grandson Jacob, along with those who have formally joined the Jewish nation and adopted the Jewish way of life. In other words, this entire passage is about the Jewish people.

God promises that his unique relationship with the nation of Israel will stand the test of time: "At that time, declares the LORD, I will be the God of all the clans of Israel, and they shall be my people" (Jeremiah 31:1). However, the most remarkable part of this prophecy is the famous "new covenant" oracle:

> Behold, the days are coming, declares the LORD, when I will make a new covenant with the house of Israel and the house of Judah, not like the covenant that I made with their fathers on the day when I took them by the hand to bring them out of the land of Egypt, my covenant that they broke, though I was their husband, declares the LORD. For this is the covenant that I will make with the house of Israel after those days, declares the LORD: I will put my

law within them, and I will write it on their hearts. And I will be their God, and they shall be my people. And no longer shall each one teach his neighbor and each his brother, saying, "Know the LORD," for they shall all know me, from the least of them to the greatest, declares the LORD. For I will forgive their iniquity, and I will remember their sin no more." (Jeremiah 31:31–34)

Consider the weight of that last statement: "I will forgive their iniquity, and I will remember their sin no more." This is the language of salvation; how can Jeremiah apply it categorically to the Jewish people? Does this mean that all Jewish people will automatically inherit eternal life?

We will have to wait until later to answer that question; this passage is indeed speaking of salvation, but not as salvation is normally understood in evangelical Christianity. This is the salvation of the entire Jewish nation; it is not a statement about the eternal destinies of individual Jews. God will forgive the corporate sin of the Jewish people—their wholesale abandonment of the Torah during the time of the kings of Israel—and he will save them from their enemies, the aggressive empires that surround them.

But when we consider the language of these prophecies, we have to conclude that there is an eternal component. For God to unilaterally promise that he will forgive the sins of the Jewish people (corporately speaking) is for God to promise the Jewish people an eternal inheritance (again, corporately speaking). After all, it is sin that separates the human race from life, from blessing, and from God himself; when sin is wiped away, so is the curse of death.

Jeremiah is not the only prophet to speak of Israel's eternal salvation. Isaiah wrote, "Israel is saved by the LORD with everlasting salvation; you shall not be put to shame or confounded to all eternity" (Isaiah 45:17).

Ezekiel penned an even more remarkable prophecy: "O house of Israel, … I will give you a new heart, and a new spirit I will put within you. And I will remove the heart of stone from your flesh and give you a heart of flesh" (Ezekiel 36:22, 26). This is the language of regeneration, the same remaking of the heart and spirit that comes to those who follow Jesus.

All these passages go on to list numerous blessings that remind us of the permanent peace that awaits God's people in the World to Come, the life hereafter. There is no ambiguity here; the Jewish people have been corporately promised forgiveness, regeneration, and eternal life—in other words, a salvation equal to what we, as followers of Jesus, anticipate for ourselves.

Paul recalls these verses and others when he writes, "They are beloved for the sake of their forefathers. For the gifts and the calling of God are irrevocable" (Romans 11:28–29), and, "All Israel will be saved" (Romans 11:26). Certainly the scope of these verses is eternal, and certainly their object is the Jewish people—the context of Romans chapters 9–11 is abundantly clear on that point.

While we are speaking of the nation of Israel in a corporate sense, we must also note in passing that for this inheritance to become a reality on a national scale, it must also become a reality for a very large number of individual Jews.

Now someone will object: aren't there other verses in the New Testament that appear to apply Jeremiah's promise to the church instead of to the Jewish people? How do we deal with those passages?

# Replacement

Traditionally-minded Christian readers may balk at my straightforward application of passages such as Jeremiah 31:31–34, the quintessential "new covenant" passage, to the Jewish people rather than to the body of Christ. When the new covenant is mentioned in the New Testament (Luke 22, 2 Corinthians 3, Hebrews 8–9), it appears to be applied exclusively to believers in Jesus.

In the next few pages I hope to demonstrate that we read these passages as applying exclusively to the church because we have inherited a certain set of assumptions. This theological viewpoint dates back to some of the earliest church fathers. Today it falls under what can loosely be defined as "replacement theology": the idea that the church has replaced the nation of Israel as God's people.

Most Christians reject the idea of replacement theology—at least, when it is presented under that name. Yet I have found that most Christians still integrate some principles of replacement theology into their theological framework—in other words, replacement theology still informs how they read and interpret the Bible.

For example, dispensationalist Christians believe that the church and Israel are two distinct (yet, in the case of Messianic Jews, overlapping) peoples of God, both of which continue to have some significance or some role to play in God's plan. Yet at the same time, the church is given a heavenly eternal destiny, while the Jewish people receive only temporal or physical blessings—for instance, the land of Israel—unless they join the church. This theology of Israel works only if some of the promises God made to Israel through the prophets are instead appropriated for the church.

Reformed theology takes a different route to what is, in the end, largely the same destination. In the Reformed theological framework, the nation of Israel never received any kind of unconditional promise or blessing from God. Rather, the numerous blessings God promised to Abraham and reiterated to his children through the prophets are thought to be directed instead toward the "elect," an undefined group within the nation of Israel. This "true spiritual Israel"[13] was revealed in the establishment of the early church, when thousands of Jews became disciples of Jesus. Only these disciples, among all the Jewish people, can participate in the covenant blessings God promised to Israel through the prophets. This theology of Israel works only if we reinterpret countless Old Testament prophetic oracles that reference the nation of Israel; we must now see them as referring to the "elect" in order to believe that the Jewish people today have no covenant standing with God outside of the curses attached to the Mosaic Law.

In both of these cases, the church is not seen as "replacing" Israel. But in dispensationalist theology, Israel is robbed of some of her promises, and in Reformed theology, she is robbed of all of them—and of course, the Christian church comes to inherit all of these promises instead. The only difference between this theology of Israel and blatant replacement theology is that in dispensationalism and Reformed theology, the Old Testament is simply retconned—a *ret*roactive *con*tinuity is established and placed over the text—to remove some or all of God's gracious promises from the nation of Israel. Israel never had the promises the prophets claimed she had; therefore, the church doesn't technically replace

Israel, but instead becomes the only group that ever inherited the gracious promises God made through the prophets.

I say this is worse than replacement theology. It is a theology that completely subverts and even erases God's election and calling of Israel. This rewriting of history is even more dangerous than the replacement theology of the early church fathers. At least Melito of Sardis and Justin Martyr had the sense to accord the people of Israel some status before God that was later taken away because of their corporate failure to enthrone Jesus as the Messiah King.[14] To read the Old Testament as if Israel never had this status to begin with is worse by an order of magnitude—not only because this reading is more subtle in its deprecation of Israel, but because this deprecation is placed at the very heart of God's relationship with Israel from the very beginning of her existence, from Abraham's call. Instead of seeing Israel forfeit all of the promises of God's coming redemption, these numerous promises are understood to hide a deeper truth, to hide God's true intent—his plan to raise up a new people, a "true spiritual Israel" to be what the Israel of the Old Testament was never actually designed to be.

In both of these widely held Christian theological systems, Israel did not just fail; she was completely set up to be nothing but a failure—the greatest patsy of all time. For thousands of years, God continually promised the Jewish people a future redemption and eternal salvation that, unbeknownst to them, was actually *for some other people*.

In my view, both dispensationalist and Reformed theology fail to make sense of the Old Testament. As we explored above, when we read prophetic oracles such as Jeremiah 30 and 31 and Ezekiel 36, they appear to be addressing the nation of Israel. Why would we not let these clear and unambiguous prophecies dictate our interpretation of the New Testament? Why wouldn't we come into the New Testament with some basic assumptions about God's eternal calling and election of Israel? Why wouldn't we assume that the human authors of the New Testament understood these Old Testament prophecies in their plain sense?

Why wouldn't we read the Bible from front to back, taking God at his word as we go?

# Reinterpretation

Let's dig in to one particular passage, Jeremiah 31:31–34, and see how a front-to-back reading of the Bible gives the reader a very different theological framework from that of replacement, dispensationalist, or Reformed theology. I want to address this passage from a few different perspectives, because in my conversations with fellow disciples of Jesus, I have found that those who object to my plain, straightforward reading of God's Old Testament promises fall into several different camps.

In one camp are those who, like me, were raised on historical-grammatical exegesis—the reader's effort to discover what each book of the Bible meant in its original setting, what its human author intended to say, and what his audience would have understood him to mean.

For those readers who share my dedication to historical-grammatical exegesis, consider the words of Walter Brueggemann on Jeremiah's new-covenant oracle:

> This oracle of promise is the best known and most relied upon of all of Jeremiah's promises. It has frequently been preempted by Christians in a supersessionist fashion, as though Jews belong to the old covenant now nullified and Christians are the sole heirs of the new covenant. ... Such a preemptive reading ignores the text itself. Moreover, such a rendering of the future could hardly be expected or cogent in the midst of these several promissory oracles which anticipate the reconstitution of the Israelite community. Such a supersessionist reading in fact asserts the rejection rather than the reconstitution of Israel, a point not on the horizon of these oracles.[15]

Brueggemann here appeals to the broader historical context of Jeremiah's prophetic oracle. Jeremiah is a Jew writing to the Jewish nation. The text is unambiguous on that point. In this light, to interpret Jeremiah 31 as referring to the church of Jesus Christ *to the exclusion of the Jewish nation* is to subvert Jeremiah's clear intention, which was to prophesy a renewed and restored nation of Israel.

This realization, drawn from a historical and grammatical interpretation of Jeremiah, raises several questions that are unanswerable in the theological systems described above. For example, if the church has replaced Israel, or if the true fulfillment of this promise will actually represent God's activity through some other group with a totally different identity and mission than Israel, then why would Jeremiah deliver this promise in the middle of a message *addressed to Israel*? Why would he stop in the middle of his effort to comfort the Jewish people in the midst of their tribulation only to promise that some future group of people, and not the Jewish people, would be the benefactors of a beautiful new covenant—a covenant that is better than the one God made with the Jewish nation? How is that helpful?

If the Jewish people were not the object of this prophecy, then was Jeremiah just rubbing salt into the raw emotional wounds of the defeated and humiliated people of Israel? Was Jeremiah actually saying, "You guys are really in a pickle here, but don't worry, because God is going to make it all better someday by *choosing somebody else*"?

How is this passage even relevant to his audience or to his readership if the group they are part of is not the group that is going to inherit the new-covenant promise?

If the community with which God will make the new covenant is so radically redefined that it excludes almost every member of the Jewish nation, how is Jeremiah's prophecy a source of comfort to its original audience, the Jewish nation? How does it fit into the rest of Jeremiah's message?

These questions will not resonate with everyone. Many Christians do not embrace historical-grammatical exegesis, especially that of the Old Testament; these include adherents of New Calvinism, whose spokespeople include Mark Driscoll and John Piper. New Calvinism represents a growing segment of evangelical Christianity that collectively embraces Reformed theology. As I have talked with New Calvinists about these questions, they have told me quite frankly that in their theological system, there is little relevance to the historical meaning of passages such as Jeremiah's new-covenant prophecy. Instead, the New Testament's reinterpretation of those passages must take priority over the apparent original meaning and over what appears to be the intent of the human author of the text.

According to New Calvinists, rather than learning about Jeremiah's historical and cultural context to find out what he meant, we should be looking at Jeremiah's prophecy through the lens of the Gospels, the letters of Paul, and the Epistle to the Hebrews—regardless of how far that interpretation may take us from the intended message of the prophet who set out to comfort the people of Israel in the midst of their exile.

To this camp I would ask, what about historical-grammatical interpretation of the New Testament? Should we understand Paul and Jesus and the author of Hebrews within their original context? Should we try to discover what they intended to communicate to their original audiences? If the answer is yes, then we must begin to pay attention to a growing body of literature that places the Gospels and Epistles firmly within first-century Judaism.

In response to this growing body of academic literature, some pastors have told me that the academic world is completely wrong about the historical person of Jesus—that he was not a practicing Jew at all, and that he really did come to overthrow a completely broken Judaism and to start a brand-new religion with a newly defined people of God. This I cannot accept; as I wrote in *Yeshua Matters*, I have seen too much evidence to the contrary.

Other pastors, who take the academic world a little more seriously, have told me that Jesus lived in a bygone age and that his teachings regarding Israel and the Torah need to be reinterpreted. I have also been told that the twelve apostles failed to understand God's redemptive program and that the book of Acts cannot be regarded as prescriptive or authoritative for Christian living—it is merely an inspired history book.

If this is true, then Paul and perhaps the author of Hebrews are the only New Testament authors left to whom we can appeal for any kind of authoritative theological direction. (Perhaps, then, we should not call ourselves Christians but Paulites.)

New Calvinists are theologically conservative. They believe that the Bible is inspired by God, or at least that this was true of the Bible's original manuscripts. On that basis I would challenge these fellow disciples of Jesus to reconsider their method of interpretation. In my opinion, we cannot believe that the entire Bible is inspired but then claim that we may only appeal to Paul among its human authors to authoritatively resolve issues of theology and praxis.

Some may appeal to "progressive revelation"—the idea that God slowly revealed more of his plan as history unfolded—to support their near-exclusive reliance on Paul, but this appeal falls flat when we realize that the oracles of Jeremiah, Ezekiel, and others must be so radically reinterpreted in the Reformed paradigm so as to make the original "revelation" meaningless. The promise of Israel's final redemption is not "progressively revealed" to have some broader meaning; rather, the apparent original meaning is overwritten with a new one that makes sense only from the perspective of a reader from the distant future.

Besides that, Paul and the author of Hebrews are not exempt from the scrutiny of scholars who increasingly suspect that both writers were in fact faithful Jews, and that their reputation as antagonists of Judaism is really undeserved. While it may be possible to believe for a little while longer that Pauline (really, Protestant) theology is the consummation of God's revelation and that it overrides and reinterprets everything that came before, it appears to me that Paul and the author of Hebrews are merely the last dominoes to fall as the New Testament is increasingly being recognized as a thoroughly Jewish collection of documents.

To go to one final extreme, if we reject historical-grammatical interpretation of the New Testament as well, and if the entire Bible has to be reinterpreted in accordance with Protestant theology in order for Protestant theology to remain coherent, I have no further argument—such a mindset is just too foreign to me. I cannot accept that all sixty-six books that make up the Bible cannot mean what they obviously meant to those who wrote them, or to those who first read them. To me, this point of view doesn't make sense. If we require such a radical reinterpretation of the Scriptures in order to confirm our theology, then we never needed the Scriptures to begin with, and in fact they have become a hindrance rather than a help.

Yet there are some theological questions that must still be answered. We cannot be so rash as to bring into question the traditional framework of evangelical soteriology, the doctrine of individual salvation (who inherits eternal life?), and ecclesiology, the doctrine of the church (who are the people of God?), without offering some answer, some alternative, some other option that may serve to more faithfully represent what God has revealed through the Scriptures. After all, just as my interpretation of Jeremiah conflicts with evangelical theology, my thesis also appears to fly in the face of several New Testament passages.

Like this one: "Whoever believes in him is not condemned, but whoever does not believe is condemned already, because he has not believed in the name of the only Son of God" (John 3:18).

Or this one: "Jesus said to him, 'I am the way, and the truth, and the life. No one comes to the Father except through me'" (John 14:6).

However, in part because of the sensitive nature of this issue, and in part because we are not really ready yet at this point in the book, I am going to wait until the final chapter to address the final destinies of individual Jewish people. I end this chapter with a reminder that the picture the prophets paint is one in which the Jewish people, *corporately speaking*, are present in the life hereafter, under a new covenant that God will make with the Jewish nation. Before we try to reconcile this idea with what the New Testament teaches about individual eternal destiny, let us place that problem on the back burner for a little while longer and explore a few more groups of people and how they are defined in the Bible.

As we do this, however, keep in mind that traditional religious Jews have understood and appropriated the above-mentioned prophecies and promises in accordance with a historical-grammatical method of interpretation. They understand that the Jewish people have a corporate inheritance in the World to Come. As a hint of what is to come in later chapters, I remind the reader that this promise does not automatically guarantee eternal life to every Jewish person (and here the New Testament and rabbinic literature agree; see Matthew 3:7–10; Romans 9; m.*Sanhedrin* 10:1–4). However, the Jewish people will be corporately represented in the World to Come on the basis of God's unilateral promises to Israel.

Should we later find a passage in the New Testament that appears to proscribe, annul, or wipe out these covenants and promises, we had better be careful in our interpretation. God does not break covenant. He does everything he says he will do. He is faithful.

# The Nations

*Therefore remember that at one time you*
*Gentiles in the flesh, called "the uncircumcision"*
*by what is called the circumcision, which is made*
*in the flesh by hands—remember that you were*
*at that time separated from Christ, alienated*
*from the commonwealth of Israel and strangers*
*to the covenants of promise, having no hope and*
*without God in the world.*

— *Ephesians 2:11–12*

In the last chapter we offered a definition of the Jewish people, along with an outline of how they came to be and what their corporate destiny looks like as promised by God through the Old Testament prophets and reaffirmed by the Apostle Paul.

So what about everyone else? What about the rest of the nations of the world?

Most people reading this book aren't Jewish. Yet most of you are believers in Jesus. If you are a non-Jewish believer in Jesus, then you have a relationship with God despite the fact that you are not a member of the historical people of God, the Jewish people. How this came to be is the subject of a later chapter. But what about before you decided to follow Jesus? What was your status in God's eyes? Was it different from that of a non-Jesus-believing Jewish person?

The answer is yes.

If everything we just read about Abraham, about the Jewish people, and about the covenants and promises of Israel is true, then those of us who are not part of that community do not share in its blessings. The covenants are divisive; they are exclusive. The covenants affect the entire world, but they do so through a specific group of called-out people, the Jewish people.

And that is not the picture of God we are used to.

The salvation story of Christianity is cosmic and universal. All mankind sinned in Adam, and the world fell into ruin. All who choose to follow Jesus are granted eternal life through his atoning death and resurrection, and through him the world will be restored. There is no distinction, no special case, no exception.

But with what we have just learned, with the Jewish people put back into the picture, things look a little different.

So what is God's plan for the nations? If God's plan for the Jewish people is based on the everlasting covenants he made with them, what is left for the other peoples of the world?

We will first answer this question with respect to those from the nations who are not part of the body of Christ. Jesus' followers are in a unique situation; the New Testament makes that very clear. But before we try to define the church of Jesus Christ, we must clearly understand the destiny that awaited us before God broke into our lives through Christ and brought us into his salvation economy.

## Favoritism

By this point, if you are still tracking with me, you may be lodging a mental accusation of favoritism toward the Almighty.

After all, God created everyone. How can he single out one group of people for special treatment—not based on their personal response to him, but based on their nationality?

A cosmic, infinite God should have a cosmic, infinite plan of salvation that places everyone on equal ground. It's just not fair to play favorites, especially when we begin to ask how membership in certain groups—the Jewish people or the body of Christ—impacts the eternal destiny of individual souls.

So stay with me when I say that in spite of what we have read in the previous chapter, God most certainly does not play favorites.

One of my favorite Bible passages, and one that I wish I had memorized much earlier, alongside John 3:16 and Romans 3:23, is Acts 10:34–35, in which the Apostle Peter says, "Truly I understand that God shows no partiality, but in every nation anyone who fears him and does what is right is acceptable to him."

Translations vary on the word "partiality," but the general meaning here is that God doesn't discriminate on the basis of nationality. God is an equal-opportunity Savior.

So he doesn't play favorites after all.

This verse appears in one of the most important chapters in the entire Bible—the chapter that records Peter's encounter with Cornelius the Gentile. According to Acts 10, a Gentile centurion named Cornelius spoke in tongues, clear evidence that God had accepted him as a candidate for membership in the body of Christ. This event may not be earth-shattering news for us today, but at the time, Cornelius' baptism was amazing and unprecedented. Until Cornelius, all of Jesus' followers had been Jewish. For all anyone knew, Jesus' followers would always be exclusively Jewish.

When Cornelius spoke in tongues, though, everything changed. The apostles began to realize that both Jews and Gentiles could be filled with the Holy Spirit and could be part of what God was doing through the body of Christ. Regardless of membership in one group or another—the Jewish nation or some other nation—individuals could be accepted by God into the body of Christ.

But I want to draw your attention to an interesting fact.

Peter received his revelation that God doesn't play favorites *before Cornelius spoke in tongues.*

Everyone who had come with Peter was surprised when the Holy Spirit descended on the Gentiles. But Peter's realization came before this occurred, when Cornelius revealed to Peter that an angel had spoken to him—before Cornelius formally joined the body of Christ.

Why did Peter come to this realization at this particular time? What had been his opinion before Acts 10? Why hadn't he expected God to move among the Gentiles in the same way he had been moving among the Jews? And why did he change his mind about Gentiles before Cornelius joined the body of Christ?

To understand the answers to these questions, we need to take a little time to explore how Jews felt and thought about the other nations of the world in the centuries and millennia before Christ.[16]

# Hostility

Nations other than Israel figure prominently in the Torah. They are mentioned often. However, it is a specific group of nations that dominates the Torah's narrative: the nations that Israel drove out of Canaan at God's command in order to take possession of the land. Those nations are portrayed negatively in the Torah. God had to remind Israel over and over that the idolatrous practices of those nations had reached such horrible depths that the inhabitants of Canaan needed to be completely destroyed.

However, those nations are a special case. When we move further into the Scripture, we get a more general view of the nations—although there is still a lot of hostility and negativity toward the nations on the part of the authors of these later Scriptures. We will focus on the negative side in this section.

The Psalms are fertile ground for this hostile attitude toward the nations:

> You have rebuked the nations; you have made the wicked perish; you have blotted out their name forever and ever. (Psalm 9:5)

> The wicked shall return to Sheol [the grave, a place of death and darkness], all the nations that forget God. (Psalm 9:17)

> The LORD is king forever and ever; the nations perish from his land. (Psalm 10:16)

> The LORD brings the counsel of the nations to nothing; he frustrates the plans of the peoples. (Psalm 33:10)

> You, LORD God of hosts, are God of Israel. Rouse yourself to punish all the nations; spare none of those who treacherously plot evil. Selah. (Psalm 59:5)

Let the high praises of God be in their throats and two-edged swords in their hands, to execute vengeance on the nations and punishments on the peoples. (Psalm 149:6–7)

The prophets of Israel also rebuked the nations:

The nations roar like the roaring of many waters, but he will rebuke them, and they will flee far away. (Isaiah 17:13)

For the LORD is enraged against all the nations, and furious against all their host; he has devoted them to destruction, has given them over for slaughter. (Isaiah 34:2)

Pour out your wrath on the nations that know you not, and on the peoples that call not on your name. (Jeremiah 10:25)

The clamor will resound to the ends of the earth, for the LORD has an indictment against the nations; he is entering into judgment with all flesh, and the wicked he will put to the sword, declares the LORD. (Jeremiah 25:31)

I will make a full end of all the nations to which I have driven you. (Jeremiah 46:28)

For the day is near, the day of the LORD is near; it will be a day of clouds, a time of doom for the nations. (Ezekiel 30:3)

After the time of the prophets but before the time of Jesus, the Jewish people continued to have conflict with the nations around them. During the time of the Maccabees, the Jewish people fought the oppressive Seleucid Empire, which tried to destroy the Jewish way of life. Later the Romans invaded and made Israel a colony. While the Romans let the Jewish people obey their ancestral customs, they also held regular public executions to remind everyone who was in charge.

The godless nations around Israel always seemed to be causing problems for the Jewish people.

Certainly Peter would have been familiar with the Scripture verses cited above; the Psalms were a regular part of Jewish worship, and sections from the Prophets were read aloud in the synagogues. He also would have known the history of the nation of Israel and the calamity she had endured at the hands of other nations. His whole life he had experienced firsthand the iron fist of Roman oppression.

We can see that many factors probably contributed to Peter's hesitation to interact with those from other nations—a major factor being the Bible itself. However, there is another stream of thought throughout the Old Testament concerning the nations of the world, and it is a stream filled with hope.

## Restoration

There is a stream of thought regarding the nations in the Psalms and in the books of the Prophets that is even more prominent than judgment and destruction. This stream is expressed in a continuing hope and promise that at some point the nations will repent of their idolatry and sin and will worship the God of Abraham.

They will do this because of how clearly God's character is revealed through the Jewish people. This character is revealed only when the nation of Israel is obedient to God and is blessed for that obedience, so prophecies regarding the ultimate restoration and repentance of the nations are often connected with prophecies of the final restoration and repentance of the Jewish people.

This hope is often expressed in the Psalms:

> All the ends of the earth shall remember and turn to the LORD, and all the families of the nations shall worship before you. (Psalm 22:27)

> I will cause your name to be remembered in all generations; therefore nations will praise you forever and ever. (Psalm 45:17)

> Be still, and know that I am God. I will be exalted among the nations, I will be exalted in the earth! (Psalm 46:10)

> May God be gracious to us and bless us and make his face to shine upon us, that your way may be known on earth, your saving power among all nations. Let the peoples praise you, O God; let all the peoples praise you! Let the nations be glad and sing for joy, for you judge the peoples with equity and guide the nations upon earth. (Psalm 67:1–4)

> All the nations you have made shall come and worship before you, O Lord, and shall glorify your name. (Psalm 86:9)

The prophets echo the same hope:

> It shall come to pass in the latter days that the mountain of the house of the LORD shall be established as the highest of the mountains, and shall be lifted up above the hills; and all the nations shall flow to it, and many peoples shall come, and say: "Come, let us go up to the mountain of the LORD, to the house of the God of Jacob, that he may teach us his ways and that we may walk in his paths." For out of Zion shall go the law, and the word of the LORD from Jerusalem. He shall judge between the nations, and shall decide disputes for many peoples; and they shall beat their swords into plowshares. (Isaiah 2:2–4)

> In that day the root of Jesse, who shall stand as a signal for the peoples—of him shall the nations inquire, and his resting place shall be glorious. (Isaiah 11:10)

> It is too light a thing that you should be my servant to raise up the tribes of Jacob and to bring back the preserved of Israel; I will make you as a light for the nations, that my salvation may reach to the end of the earth. (Isaiah 49:6)

> For at that time I will change the speech of the peoples to a pure speech, that all of them may call upon the name of the LORD and serve him with one accord. (Zephaniah 3:9)

> In those days ten men from the nations of every tongue shall take hold of the robe of a Jew, saying, "Let us go with you, for we have heard that God is with you." (Zechariah 8:23)

> For from the rising of the sun to its setting my name will be great among the nations, and in every place incense will be offered to my name, and a pure offering. (Malachi 1:11)

It seems strange to place these passages alongside those that prophesy the judgment and destruction—sometimes even total destruction—of the nations. Yet both of these ideas are frequently repeated in the Old Testament.

What is going on here? What does God have planned for the nations of the world?

## Standards

An even more pressing question might be, according to what standard, or law, will God judge the nations?

This is a critical question, because in the time of Jesus, Peter, and the rest of the apostles, God had clearly revealed himself only to the Jewish people.

When the children of Israel failed to keep the laws God had given them, they were judged; when they were diligent to keep the laws of God, they were blessed. But this arrangement worked only because God had revealed all these laws to the Jewish people on Mount Sinai.

Psalm 147:19–20 states, "He declares his word to Jacob, his statutes and rules to Israel. He has not dealt thus with any other nation; they do not know his rules." So how can the nations of the world be held accountable to God? To what standard are they held? What rules are they expected to follow? And how can God judge them for not following these rules if there is no way for them to know what the rules are?

The solution to this problem in Jewish thought was not to posit, as Christian theologians do, that everyone is automatically sinful from the time they are conceived and therefore automatically condemned, no matter what. There is no "original sin" in Judaism. Rather, the Apostle Paul repeats a commonly held Jewish belief regarding the nations in Romans chapter 1:

> For the wrath of God is revealed from heaven against all ungodliness and unrighteousness of men, who by their unrighteousness suppress the truth. For what can be known about God is plain to them, because God has shown it to them. For his invisible attributes, namely, his eternal power and divine nature, have been clearly perceived, ever since the creation of the world, in the things that have been made. So they are without excuse. For although they knew God, they did not honor him as God or give thanks to him, but they became futile in

their thinking, and their foolish hearts were darkened. Claiming to be wise, they became fools, and exchanged the glory of the immortal God for images resembling mortal man and birds and animals and creeping things.

Therefore God gave them up in the lusts of their hearts to impurity, to the dishonoring of their bodies among themselves, because they exchanged the truth about God for a lie and worshiped and served the creature rather than the Creator, who is blessed forever! Amen. (Romans 1:18–25)

Paul's argument here is that the nations of the world should recognize that God exists based on the simple observation that other things exist. To Paul it seems obvious that a Creator God must exist and that this God cannot be a created or physical object, like an idol, but must be transcendent, above and beyond creation in some way.

Along with other Jews of his day, Paul believed that when a nation ignored the evidence of a transcendent God and began to worship created idols, its collective desires began to change. Idolatry was the root of the other sins of the nations; in particular it led to sexual immorality of all kinds.

Because in Paul's time all non-Jewish nations of the world had abandoned God in favor of idol worship, they were all under judgment—not necessarily in terms of the final destinies of each individual member of these nations, but in a more temporal and corporate sense. Just as the nation of Israel was conquered by other nations when she abandoned the Law of Moses, so the idol-worshiping nations had opened themselves up to natural disasters, wars, and other calamities—even up to total destruction, as in the case of the Canaanites—because of their corporate failure to respond to the natural revelation Paul refers to in Romans 1: the existence of an invisible Creator God, logically inferred from the existence of a visible creation.

However, when God decides the final destinies of individual members of the nations, he will not unilaterally condemn them because of their national affiliation. Instead, he will judge them by whether or not they personally embraced idolatry and the lifestyle that came with it. This is demonstrated in Romans 2, as Paul continues his train of thought:

> Because of your hard and impenitent heart you are storing up wrath for yourself on the day of wrath when God's righteous judgment will be revealed. He will render to each one according to his works: to those who by patience in well-doing seek for glory and honor and immortality, he will give eternal life; but for those who are self-seeking and do not obey the truth, but obey unrighteousness, there will be wrath and fury. There will be tribulation and distress for every human being who does evil, the Jew first and also the Greek, but glory and honor and peace for everyone who does good, the Jew first and also the Greek. For God shows no partiality. (Romans 2:5–11)

Paul here echoes Peter's claim that God does not show partiality, or favoritism, toward the Jewish people. He adds that both individual Jews and individual Gentiles must "by patience in well-doing seek for glory and honor and immortality" if they hope to inherit the happy and blessed afterlife that God has promised to his people. Whether they are members of a corporate group that is in covenant with God (the Jewish people) or a corporate group that is estranged from God (the idolatrous nations), individuals will be held accountable for their own actions when Christ sits down to judge and decide their eternal destinies.

While foreign to evangelical theology, the idea that both Jews and Gentiles who strive for righteousness will be acceptable to God is the dominant Jewish view of final destinies,[17] and Paul embraces it as a key part of his argument in Romans.

With this in mind, let's return to Cornelius in Acts 10 and find out why Peter made the revealing statement that God shows no partiality.

## God-Fearer

Cornelius is described in Acts 10 in a few short phrases. These phrases, however, reveal a lot about the kind of person Cornelius was.

First, Cornelius is said to be "a devout man who feared God with all his household" (Acts 10:2). A "man who feared God," or "God-fearer," was a well-understood designation in first-century Judaism.[18] God-fearers were non-Jews, Gentiles, who attached themselves to the God of Abraham. They may have had some relationship with a local synagogue. They often prayed facing the Temple at the times of the Temple sacrifices (a Jewish custom still practiced today). They gave money to the synagogue and to poverty-stricken Jews.

Cornelius is described as just such a person. He "gave alms generously to the people"—that is, to the Jewish community. He also "prayed continually to God," a reference to the practice of praying at the set times of prayer in Judaism. In fact, the time the angel appeared to Cornelius, "the ninth hour of the day" (Acts 10:3), was the time of the afternoon sacrifice and a set time of prayer (see Acts 3:1).

It is interesting to note that Cornelius was also a centurion, a high-ranking Roman soldier (Acts 10:1). Centurions would have been required to take part in some of the idolatrous rituals of Rome; emperor worship was closely connected with service in the legions.[19] We don't know whether Cornelius personally took part in these rituals or instead found a way around them. However, many or even most God-fearers would have engaged in idolatrous rituals, since often to refuse to do so would have meant severe penalties or even death at the hands of their countrymen. Participation in cultic worship was a mandatory civic responsibility.[20]

Think about how a pious Jew would have regarded a person like Cornelius. Obviously, Cornelius was a great guy, and he had a good reputation. A lot of people knew about his generosity, and they knew he worshiped the God of Abraham (Acts 10:22). But even knowing this, Peter reflected that it was "unlawful," that is, against Jewish tradition, to associate with Cornelius.

Peter references a tradition to the effect that Jews were not at that time even allowed go into a Gentile's house (Acts 10:28). Why was this the case? With everything we know about Cornelius, why would Peter still be breaking from Jewish tradition to enter his house?

Because the issue at hand was not holiness or the pursuit of righteousness on the part of the individual, in this case Cornelius.

Instead, Peter's reluctance reflected the fact that Peter and Cornelius were on two different sides of the dividing line between Jew and Gentile. Peter was in a group that was in covenant with God, and Cornelius was in a group that had abandoned God.

Don't forget that, in the ancient world, the Jewish people were the only nation that collectively acknowledged the living God, the God of the Bible. As a result, by the time of the apostles, Jewish tradition had developed certain rules about interacting with Gentiles based on the reality that all other nations worshiped idols. These rules applied across the board to every Gentile; that's just the way they were designed. So even though Cornelius the Gentile was doing what he could to worship the God of Israel, he fell into the same legal category as the rest of the Gentiles, members of the idol-worshiping nations that God was going to judge in the last days.

Categorically speaking, it was a safe assumption that Gentiles—even God-fearers—were idolatrous, that their food was polluted by idols, and that their houses had been rendered unclean through pagan burial practices.[21] Because of this reality, in order to remain faithful to their dietary laws and to remain in a state of ritual purity, Jewish people simply could not closely associate with Gentiles.

Because of the great difficulty it presented for an observant Jew to have social relationships with non-Jews, Peter may have assumed that God was solely interested in working among the Jewish people—at least as far as the ministry of the body of Christ was concerned. After all, how could Gentiles, who were idolaters by definition, become a part of the holy people that God had called out to be the body of the Messiah?

Paul later wrote that food contaminated by idols could have no place at the table at which the disciples of Jesus ate together (1 Corinthians 10:20–22). Even this tangential contact with idolatry, which had no connection with any evil or idolatrous intent on the part of those who ate, was enough to tarnish the holiness of the body of Christ.[22]

To reiterate, the Jewish people were unequivocally the only nation that recognized the God of Abraham as the one true God. This being the case, as God called out a group of people to form the *ekklesia*, the assembly, the church of Jesus Christ, how could people from other nations—idolatrous nations—join in as undifferentiated members? How could Cornelius, neck-deep in the Emperor's legions and a participant in all that legion service entailed, sit at table with the disciples of Jesus without bringing that impurity with him?

Peter, however, had something new to consider when he learned that an angel had appeared to Cornelius. When he heard Cornelius tell his story, immediately he responded, "Truly I understand that God shows no partiality, but in every nation anyone who fears him and does what is right is acceptable to him" (Acts 10:34–35).

In other words, before Cornelius received the Holy Spirit as evidence of his eligibility for membership in the body of Christ, Peter acknowledged that Cornelius had some standing before God. Despite being a member of a corporate group that worshiped idols, Cornelius was acceptable to God because he had responded to God's call on his life; he had responded to the truth that God had revealed to him. He had, on the whole, personally rejected idolatry and sin as much as he possibly could in his situation. He was generous in caring for the poor. He was not part of the people of Israel, and as such was not part of the people of God, but he had made every effort to join in the worship of the God of Abraham alongside the Jewish community.

Cornelius's visitation from an angel indicated to Peter that individual Gentiles, even members of categorically idolatrous nations, could live in a way that was pleasing to God by personally rejecting idolatry and sin and by responding to God's call—whatever that call might look like. For Cornelius it had meant embracing a life of submission to the God of Israel and to his laws. With Peter's arrival at his house and the revelation of the gospel message, God's call to Cornelius took on a new and sharper form; Cornelius was called to become a disciple of Rabbi Jesus of Nazareth, above and beyond the acts of piety he had already been accustomed to. Corporately speaking, he shifted from being a member of an idolatrous nation to a member of the body of Christ.

As a result of the Cornelius event, Peter may have begun to reconsider the many Old Testament prophets and psalms that spoke of a future redemption for those among the nations who repented and came to the Jewish people for knowledge about the living God. Perhaps he began to see that these prophecies were coming true before his eyes through the ministry of Jesus Christ, as non-Jews personally repented of their sins and responded to God's call to become disciples of Jesus.

But Peter also clearly understood that God could work in the hearts of individual Gentiles who had not yet heard of Jesus Christ. These Gentiles were not part of any group that had a corporate relationship with God. Yet in spite of that, they could become acceptable to God by responding to his personal call on their lives.[23]

## Destiny

So what is the destiny of the nations?

In first-century Jewish thought, which was based on the Old Testament, the nations were corporately under judgment because they had abandoned God to worship idols. As for individual Gentiles, those members of the nations who embraced idolatry and the sinful lifestyle that came with it were to be judged and condemned by God at some future time.

On the other hand, Jewish theology to this day embraces the idea that those individual Gentiles who reject idolatry and the sins that come with it will inherit eternal blessing, despite the fact that they are not part of any group that has a corporate relationship with God. As Peter said, "Truly I understand that God shows no partiality, but in every nation anyone who fears him and does what is right is acceptable to him" (Acts 10:34–35). Again, as Paul argued in Romans 2:10–11, there will be "glory and honor and peace for everyone who does good, the Jew first and also the Greek. For God shows no partiality."

However, the apostles also clearly taught that only in Christ will this glory and honor and peace finally be realized. Without the gospel the hope of eternal life is completely hidden, even from those Gentiles who have begun to respond to God's call and who are seeking to do good despite never having received the revelation of the Law of Moses. These Gentiles have no knowledge of God's mercy and salvation. They have no reason to hope for a better life hereafter, because they are separated from the people to whom God revealed all these things. Whatever their final destiny might be, they are unable to become part of the visible kingdom of heaven in this life because they are disconnected from God's people. They are not party to God's gracious covenants and promises.

Paul reflects this sentiment in Ephesians 2:11–12:

> Therefore remember that at one time you Gentiles in
> the flesh, called "the uncircumcision" by what is called
> the circumcision, which is made in the flesh by hands—
> remember that you were at that time separated from
> Christ, alienated from the commonwealth of Israel and
> strangers to the covenants of promise, having no hope
> and without God in the world.

Here the distinction between corporate salvation and individual destiny is very sharp. The nations of the world as corporate entities have no covenant standing before God. They have no formal relationship to God. They are promised no corporate salvation. In fact, they are promised judgment for their corporate abandonment of God. Yet this does not mean that every person who lives or has ever lived in these nations will be categorically condemned and forever excluded from God's presence. According to Peter, every individual from among the nations "who fears him and does what is right" will find that they are acceptable to God at the final judgment.

Now to base our view of the final destinies of non-Jesus-believing Gentiles on Romans 1 and 2 and on Peter's revealing statement in Acts 10 is to depart in a significant way from evangelical Christian theology. To say that Gentiles who strive to do good will be accepted by God sounds suspiciously like works-based salvation, which runs deeply against the grain of Protestant theology—though many theologians have argued, as would I, that God's grace, rather than human works or merit, is really the decisive factor at work here.[24]

However, we will yet again set the question of individual eternal destiny on the back burner as we continue to explore the major groups of people defined in the Bible and their corporate relationships to God. In this chapter we are only trying to discover what the Bible says about the corporate destiny of the nations of the world in order to contrast this destiny with that of the nation of Israel. We have established that, according to the Old Testament, no other nation has a corporate relationship with God as Israel does. As to the eternal destinies of individual Gentiles, some from among the nations will be judged and condemned by God, while others will be saved. This decision will be based on how they have lived their lives and the choices they have made. This was, generally speaking, Jewish thought on the destiny of the nations in the time of Jesus.

In the next chapter we will dive back into the New Testament and begin to see how these concepts were understood and applied by the apostles, and how they formed some of the building blocks of the early Christian message. Where we end up will not be so far from normative Christian theology as you might think. But we have to get there by the right path; we have to lay this foundation first.

# The Church

*So then you are no longer strangers and aliens,
but you are fellow citizens with the saints and
members of the household of God, built on
the foundation of the apostles and prophets,
Christ Jesus himself being the cornerstone,
in whom the whole structure, being joined
together, grows into a holy temple in the Lord.
In him you also are being built together into
a dwelling place for God by the Spirit.*

— *Ephesians 2:19–22*

So what about those of us who follow Jesus? How do we fit? Where do we stand in relationship to the two people groups we have just explored—the nation of Israel and the other nations of the world?

Building on the foundation we have just laid, we can come up with an answer that makes a lot of sense—however, it may be slightly different from the answer many of us grew up with. Traditionally, the church has not defined itself in light of God's covenant relationship with the Jewish people. Instead, the church has simply taken Old Testament prophecies of blessing, peace, and eternal life and reinterpreted them exclusively to the benefit of believers in Jesus.

This doesn't work. As we argued in an earlier chapter, these promises and prophecies are very clearly directed at the Jewish people. God has used every possible wording to make this clear: "My people, Israel and Judah" (Jeremiah 30:3), "all the clans of Israel" (Jeremiah 31:1), "the house of Israel and the house of Judah" (Jeremiah 31:31), and "the offspring of Israel" (Jeremiah 31:36)—and all that just in one passage.

We must ask ourselves, how much more specific would God need to be in order to communicate to us that these promises and prophecies were directed toward the Jewish people?

But if these promises were not given to Gentiles, then how do Gentile followers of Jesus relate to them? If we are not part of the Jewish people, how are we part of the people of God? And as individuals, how do we inherit eternal life if God's covenants were made only with the Jewish people? What exactly are we, and how do we fit into all these prophecies?

Before we try to answer to that question, let's look at how another theologian has answered it—and why I think his answers don't quite fit the evidence.

## Reduction

This book and the rest of the books in the *Matters* series are not academic books, but they are all based on ideas supported by published scholarship. There aren't too many pastors out there teaching that Jesus and the apostles, even Paul, continued to self-identify as faithful, practicing Jews; but scholars from many different backgrounds have thrown their weight behind this idea. Within two schools of thought, broadly called the "Third Quest for the Historical Jesus" and the "Radical New Perspective on Paul," dozens of researchers, theologians, and academics now champion the Jewish Jesus and his Jewish disciples.[25]

Some of these ideas have percolated into magazines and onto bookstore shelves in the writings of N.T. Wright, former bishop of Durham and a prolific author—and a great scholar in his own right. N.T. Wright has built an interesting, refreshing, and highly engaging theological system that attempts to take into account many of the historical factors we have discussed. He is acutely aware of the social divide that existed between Jews and Gentiles in the first century and how the apostles negotiated that divide. He has also pioneered the idea that the concepts of forgiveness, salvation, and redemption are normally used corporately in the Bible—that is, they are often used of groups of people and not usually of individuals. Wright has been on the front end of research in these areas; in fact, he was one of a few Christian theologians proposing "a new perspective" on Paul before that term was made popular by another scholar, James D. G. Dunn.[26]

I enjoy and respect N.T. Wright, and I have a lot of his books. The distinction I make in this book between corporate salvation and the final destinies of individuals is drawn heavily from his research. However, I differ from him in this critical area of how God's covenants and promises to the Jewish people should shape the identity of the church, the body of believers in Christ.

For N.T. Wright, all the promises and covenants between God and the Jewish people were summed up in Christ.[27] Though I may not do justice to his theology by abbreviating it in this way, I understand him to teach that the destiny of the Jewish people is found solely in the person of Jesus. The promises of eternal life, an eternal inheritance, eternal blessing—only Jesus, among all his brethren, has received these things, because only he was completely and totally faithful to the Law of Moses, and because he is able to sum up the identity of the entire nation as the Messiah King.

Those who believe in Jesus can participate in these covenants and promises. Those of us who have dedicated our lives to Jesus are "in Christ," and in him we inherit all the blessings God promised to Abraham and to his descendants. No one else, not even the Jewish nation, obtains these blessings. If this sounds familiar, that's because this is the classical Christian definition of who is and who is not part of God's people. Wright may get to this position by a different route, but his destination is the same. It is, for all intents and purposes, replacement theology.

N.T. Wright's theology relies heavily on the letters of Paul. Much of the language he uses is drawn directly from Paul. But I don't want to try to refute him on that ground. Instead, I want to recall the language God used when he made covenants and promises with the Jewish people. How, in any way, can "all the clans of Israel" (Jeremiah 31:1) be redefined so radically as to exclude the vast majority of Jewish people? How can such a prophecy as "You shall dwell in the land that I gave to your fathers, and you shall be my people, and I will be your God" (Ezekiel 36:28) refer to anyone else but the physical people of Israel?

It is true that Jesus sums up the identity of his people.[28] In some way he represents the entire Jewish nation as their Messiah King. But as he *takes on* the identity of the Jewish nation, does he also *remove* the identity of God's covenant people from the Jewish nation? In other words, does Jesus leverage his identity as the consummate Jew to strip away God's promises and covenants from the nation of Israel?

Imagine that you have categorically promised a silver dollar to each of your great-grandchildren. You write out the promise so that everyone will see it: "I will give all my great-grandchildren silver dollars."

Imagine that you wrote this promise during a time in which your children and grandchildren had abandoned you, a time during which you were separated from them. (Many of the promises God made to the Jewish people were made during the exile, a time of punishment and national estrangement from God.)

Now imagine that on your deathbed you gather all your great-grandchildren around. You produced a large family and taught your children to do the same, so over one hundred of your descendants are packed into the room. You pull out a box of silver dollars and say, "You—the one on the left. You can have all the silver dollars I promised now. Do whatever you want with them."

One of your other grandchildren would undoubtedly respond, "Wait a minute. That's not what you promised."

## Vindication

Obviously, the allegory breaks down if we take it too far. N.T. Wright believes that all the Jewish people *can* attain salvation—all the great-grandchildren can get silver dollars. But they have to get it by being "in Christ," which they are not unless they leave Judaism behind and join the visible body of Christ, the Christian church.

But as we read Jeremiah 30 and 31, Ezekiel 36, and other prophecies about the national destiny of the Jewish people, we find that they contain many unconditional, unilateral promises. God doesn't say, "As long as they follow the prophet I send," or, "As long as they heed my message for them in the end times," or, "As long as they are perfectly obedient."

In fact, the opposite is true. Although the Jewish people do in fact have to follow the prophet God sends, and they do have to obey the Torah, God recognizes that his people will not be able to do these things on their own. Yet he promises to save them in spite of what they have done and in spite of what they have failed to do—not for their sake but for the sake of his name, his reputation. He will save the Jewish people, because if he doesn't, his covenant with Abraham will be broken. And everyone will know it. He will be called a liar, a weakling, and a promise-breaker.

So he says:

> It is not for your sake, O house of Israel, that I am about to act, but for the sake of my holy name. ... I will vindicate the holiness of my great name. ... And the nations will know that I am the LORD, declares the Lord GOD, when through you I vindicate my holiness before their eyes. I will take you from the nations and gather you from all the countries and bring you into your own land. I will sprinkle clean water on you, and you shall be clean from all your uncleannesses, and from all your idols I will cleanse you. And I will give you a new heart, and a new spirit I will put within you. (Ezekiel 36:22–26)

God's vindication is a common theme in the prophetic books of the Old Testament. When the nations see the fortunes of the Jewish people restored against all odds, then everyone will know that the God of Israel is both powerful and gracious. They will know that he keeps covenant with his people, despite their shortcomings and faults.

And while under the Law of Moses, the Jewish people must repent of their sins and obey God completely in order to gain the full blessings of God's covenants, God has found a way around that restriction: "I will put my Spirit within you, and cause you to walk in my statutes and be careful to obey my rules" (Ezekiel 36:27). God will cause the Jewish people to obey him so that he can bless and restore them.

Part of this obedience will be Israel's acceptance of Jesus as the Messiah. In *Yeshua Matters* we explained that Jesus was a prophet. To be more specific, he was a unique prophet about whom Moses told the Jewish people, as recorded in Deuteronomy 18:15–19. Moses warned the people that they would be required to listen to this prophet—Jesus—and obey his message. Because the Jewish people corporately, as one unified group, have not done this, many Christians believe that God is finished with them.

But because we know that God has promised to turn the hearts of the Jewish people toward repentance, I think we must assume that they *will* someday see Jesus for who he is. God will open their eyes. The Jewish people will accept Jesus as the Messiah, and they will obey Jesus' message, a message of love and the eradication of baseless hatred, a message of repentance and humble reconciliation to God, a message of caring for the poor and the needy, and a message that all who respond to him in repentance and faith can be part of God's kingdom in this world and in the World to Come.

The acceptance of Jesus the Messiah and his prophetic message will be a necessary step in the redemption of the Jewish people. Jesus spoke to the very things that needed to be repaired in order for the Jewish people to be completely restored. So the Jewish people absolutely need Jesus. Only when his message is heard and obeyed will God finally and permanently rescue his people—again, not every individual person but the group as a whole. We know that this must eventually happen, because God has promised exactly that through the prophets.

I cannot accept that all these promises have found their final realization solely in Jesus and in his followers, a category that excludes most Jewish people. "All the clans of Israel" must see the fruit of these promises in order for God's name to be vindicated. As such, the redemption of the Jewish people is guaranteed to happen, because God's holy name *must* be vindicated.

While Jesus may be the only Jewish person to truly deserve God's covenant blessings, he is going to leverage his position as the Messiah King to take the rest of his people under his wings. He will do this in order to fulfill God's promises to them, which will in turn magnify God's reputation among the rest of the nations of the world, which know about these promises and are waiting to see what God will do.

Paul revealed this part of God's redemptive plan in his Epistle to the Romans:

> For I tell you that Christ became a servant to the circumcised [the Jewish people] to show God's truthfulness, in order to confirm the promises given to the patriarchs, and in order that the Gentiles might glorify God for his mercy. As it is written, "Therefore I will praise you among the Gentiles, and sing to your name." (Romans 15:8–9)

The world will see the Jewish people restored through Jesus Christ. Everyone will know that God keeps his promises when they see the promises he made to the patriarchs fulfilled. Everyone will know that God is merciful and keeps covenant even when his people do not do everything he asks of them. In response to this outpouring of mercy, the nations of the world will glorify God for what he has done for his people.

After all, he is no promise-breaker.

# Called

If the church does not automatically receive all the blessings that God promised to the Jewish people, then what do we receive and why? Into what category do we fall?

These are the very questions that began to arise within the early Jesus movement after Peter's encounter with Cornelius. It was clear to Peter and the rest of the apostles that they were seeing the beginning of the fulfillment of God's promises to redeem and restore the Jewish people. However, it was not immediately clear what role Gentile believers in Jesus had to play in all that.

At a council called to address this question, the Apostle James, the brother of Jesus Christ, quoted a verse from the prophet Amos that he felt described the movement of Gentiles to follow the Messiah and King of the Jews: "After this I will return, and I will rebuild the tent of David that has fallen; I will rebuild its ruins, and I will restore it, that the remnant of mankind may seek the Lord, and all the Gentiles who are called by my name, says the LORD, who makes these things known from of old" (Acts 15:16–18, quoting Amos 9:11–12).

When James heard that non-Jews were beginning to follow Jesus and that they had received the Holy Spirit, indicating that they were full-fledged members of the Jesus community, he must have begun to search his memory for Bible prophecies that would point to such a phenomenon.

Amos 9:11–12 is one such prophecy. In this oracle Amos foretells the restoration of the ancient monarchy, the kingdom of Israel, the throne of David. Calling it "David's fallen tent," the passage states that this line of kings will be restored in the last days. At the time of this restoration, a group of people will emerge from the nations and attach itself to Israel and to her King. These people are not Jewish, but nonetheless they are "called by [God's] name."

James connected the dots between the resurrected King Jesus, this emerging group of Gentiles who chose to follow him, and the prophecy of Amos.

The church fits the description in Amos neatly. Besides those one would naturally expect to follow the King of the Jews—Jewish people—there is another group that has come alongside them—that is, Jesus-believing Gentiles. Non-Jewish Christians.

Non-Jewish Christians fulfill many of the prophecies we quoted in the last chapter, which describe people from the nations repenting of their sins and coming to the Jewish people and their King to learn about and follow the God of Abraham (again, see Isaiah 2:2–4, 11:10, and Zechariah 8:23). We have been called from among all the nations of the world to follow the King of the Jews. However, our identity as Gentiles—as members of the nations—does not change. Indeed, it would be a shame if it did change. Our role as representatives of all the nations under heaven is a necessary and prophetic role with huge ramifications for God's kingdom and his plan to restore the entire world.

## Danger

While Peter was the first apostle to minister to Gentiles (Acts 15:7), Paul was the one who eventually took that mission worldwide.

In fact, he made an agreement with the other apostles that they would continue to minister to the Jewish people, while he took the good news of Jesus out to Gentiles across the known world (Galatians 2:6–10).

As Gentiles joined the Jesus movement, numerous problems arose. Many of these problems had to do with identity. The apostles all agreed that Gentiles could join the body of Christ without becoming Jewish:

> It has seemed good to the Holy Spirit and to us to lay on you no greater burden than these requirements: that you abstain from what has been sacrificed to idols, and from blood, and from what has been strangled, and from sexual immorality. If you keep yourselves from these, you will do well. (Acts 15:28–29)

But not everyone in the Jesus movement was comfortable with this position. Many Jews, even some Jewish believers in Jesus, were not comfortable seeing Gentiles accepted into a Jewish movement following a Jewish rabbi. After all, the nation of Israel was at that time the only category into which the people of God had ever fallen. Based on this conviction, these Jews, many of them Jesus-believing Pharisees, began to pressure Gentile believers in Jesus to undergo proselyte conversion—to become Jewish.

Many of Paul's letters address this problem. At least one, Galatians, was written solely to confront this problem.[29] Paul dissuaded—actually, forbade—the non-Jewish members of his churches from becoming Jewish through formal proselyte conversion.

Remember the prophecies about Gentiles following the King of the Jews? About Gentiles coming to the Jewish people and asking to be taught about the God of Abraham? The twelve apostles understood that the Jesus movement represented the fulfillment of these prophecies. As such, the Gentiles who were attaching themselves to Jesus added to his credibility as the Messiah King; Jesus was bringing about the repentance of the nations, just as the Messiah had been prophesied to do.

However, if all the non-Jewish followers of Jesus became Jewish, there would be no "Gentiles who are called by [God's] name" (Acts

15:17). These prophecies would fall flat. The Jesus movement would be seen as just another Jewish sect following another Jewish rabbi.

This would have been a comfortable and safe position for the Jesus movement to take. In the time of the apostles, it was actually illegal not to participate in Roman cultic worship—idol worship. While the Romans let each nation they conquered worship their own ancestral gods, everyone also had to worship the Roman gods—and particularly Caesar himself.

The Jewish people had a legal exception to this rule. Because their God was so jealous and forbade the worship of any other, and because their religious system was older than Rome's, they were allowed to continue worshiping in the way they always had. So Jews in the Jesus movement were safe as long as they were still recognized as Jews by the Roman authorities. They didn't have to follow the Roman laws about worshiping Caesar.

But Gentiles in the Jesus movement had to abandon their civic duty and stop worshiping idols in order to be part of the body of Christ. Because they weren't Jewish, it was dangerous for them to stop participating in the cultic rites of Rome. If they were discovered, the consequences could be disastrous.

Disastrous not just for them—but for the Jewish community too. The Jews did not take their special exception from idol worship lightly, and they knew that Caesar could take that exemption away—an action that would almost certainly spark armed conflict between Judea and Rome.

It is easy to imagine how having a bunch of non-Jews join a Jewish sect without converting to Judaism would draw a disapproving eye from the Roman government. It was widely thought that when a god's people failed to perform the required rites of worship, the god became angry; the peace between gods and men was broken, and disasters of all kinds resulted. Because these Gentiles were not Jewish, they were still thought to be obligated to these pagan gods; because they refused to perform the cultic rites, they could easily be blamed for any calamity that fell on the Roman Empire or its dominions. In the eyes of their pagan countrymen, these apostates had incurred the wrath of the gods by abandoning their ancestral rites of worship.[30]

While these Gentiles were certainly a fulfillment of Bible prophecy, what they were doing was dangerous, illegal, and liable to start a war between Romans and Jews—or at least to bring some kind of police action down on the Jewish community. It certainly wouldn't have been the first time. We know from history that it wouldn't have been the last, either.

## Distinction

However, despite the danger, the apostles didn't budge. They maintained their position at all costs. Consequently, Gentile Christians across the Roman Empire found themselves in a difficult position. They could not join with their countrymen and communities in idol worship, but neither could they officially join the Jewish community by adopting Jewish identity and legal status. They were stuck in an in-between place. A dangerous place.

This helps us to understand why Paul had to continually write and encourage these fledgling churches. He reiterated in many of his epistles that Gentile disciples of Jesus were an important and vital part of what God was doing, and that they needed to remain Gentiles in order to continue playing their critical role.

He laid out his position clearly in his first letter to the Corinthians:

> Let each person lead the life that the Lord has assigned to him, and to which God has called him. This is my rule in all the churches. Was anyone at the time of his call already circumcised? Let him not seek to remove the marks of circumcision. Was anyone at the time of his call uncircumcised? Let him not seek circumcision. For neither circumcision counts for anything nor uncircumcision, but keeping the commandments of God. (1 Corinthians 7:17–19)

A few chapters ago we established that, in first-century Jewish culture, "circumcision" meant "Jewishness" or "conversion to Judaism," and "uncircumcision" meant "Gentile-ness" or "to live as a Gentile"—that is, to stop following Jewish traditions, to leave the Jewish community.

Paul's "rule in all the churches" was that if someone was a Gentile when he joined the body of Christ, he was to remain a

Gentile.[31] He was not allowed to become Jewish. He must brave the danger and embrace the perilous existence of the in-between life, not having the social support network of either the broader Jewish community or the pagan Roman community.[32]

## Participants

While I do not think that all the blessings of Abraham passed over the Jewish people in favor of Jesus and his followers, I do believe along with N.T. Wright that being "in Christ" (2 Corinthians 5:17) is an important, central, and defining concept for the Christian. But it must be understood correctly.

As we have established, Gentiles who follow Jesus don't become Jewish. So being "in Christ" doesn't mean we become exactly like him, or that everything that is true about Jesus becomes true about us. We don't become Jewish any more than we become carpenters, rabbis, or gods.

So what does it mean to be "in Christ"?

As Gentiles, members of the apostate nations of the world, we have no promises that God will redeem and restore us corporately, as the Jewish people do. But Jesus does inherit these promises and covenants, because he is Jewish. And while I disagree with N.T. Wright when he says that Jesus is the only Jewish person who has received the blessings of these covenants by virtue of his Jewishness, I do believe that Jesus, because of his extraordinary mission and the unique office he holds, can extend some of these covenant blessings to those outside the Jewish people—to Gentiles, members of other nations.

As God said of Jesus through the Prophet Isaiah, "It is too light a thing that you should be my servant to raise up the tribes of Jacob and to bring back the preserved of Israel; I will make you as a light for the nations, that my salvation may reach to the end of the earth" (Isaiah 49:6).

How was this possible? Isaiah goes on later in the same oracle to explain:

> Behold, my servant shall act wisely; he shall be high and
> lifted up, and shall be exalted. As many were astonished
> at you—his appearance was so marred, beyond human

semblance, and his form beyond that of the children of mankind—so shall he sprinkle many nations; kings shall shut their mouths because of him; for that which has not been told them they see, and that which they have not heard they understand. (Isaiah 52:13–15)

Isaiah proceeds to describe the death of the servant, whom we now know to be Jesus Christ. According to Isaiah, "Out of the anguish of his soul he shall see and be satisfied; by his knowledge shall the righteous one, my servant, make many to be accounted righteous, and he shall bear their iniquities" (Isaiah 53:11).

Jesus, because he was completely righteous and yet died on our behalf, is able to cause us to be accounted righteous. As we discussed above, it is our sins that keep us from being able to inherit eternal life. When we dedicate our lives to Jesus, we are accounted righteous because of him.

Therefore, it can be truly said that "in Christ" we are righteous. "In Christ" we are a new creation; we receive the new heart and new spirit that God promised to the Jewish people in Ezekiel 36:26.

It is not immediately obvious which of the Old Testament's covenant blessings are extended to Jesus' non-Jewish disciples. We simply have to read the New Testament and discover the specifics for ourselves. We cannot categorically say that we receive all of them. But eternal life (John 3:16), a place in the World to Come (John 14:3), the forgiveness of sins (Ephesians 1:7), being made righteous (Romans 5:19), peace with God (Romans 5:1), and a personal relationship with the Almighty (Romans 8:14–17) are all included in the blessings we receive "in Christ." We will be resurrected on the last day, and we will enjoy the Messianic Age along with the redeemed Jewish people.

But wait a minute. Corporately speaking, we are still members of the idolatrous nations of the world, which are under judgment for their failure to recognize and seek out the Creator God. It is easy to say that we become individual exceptions to this judgment when we join ourselves to the person of Jesus Christ. But what about our corporate identity? If we don't become members of the Jewish nation, then do we become members of a new group? Surely we have some corporate identity besides merely being members of the apostate nations of the world.

Explaining our salvation in personal terms is easy, especially for an evangelical Christian who is used to seeing salvation from an individual perspective. But explaining it in corporate terms is a bit harder, especially when we are used to the very personal and intimate idea of salvation embraced within evangelical theology. Before we delve into categories again, then, we must introduce one more concept.

## Kingdom

By following Jesus his Gentile disciples enter the "kingdom of heaven."

The "kingdom of heaven," or "kingdom of God," is a term used throughout the New Testament to describe the place, time, or person over which God's reign and rule was manifest, or obvious—able to be seen.

The ultimate manifestation of the kingdom of God is the coming Messianic Age, in which the King of the Jews—Jesus—will reign in Jerusalem, and all nations will come to the Jewish Messiah and to his people to learn about the God of Israel (Isaiah 2:2–4).

The kingdom of God is also manifest in the supernal realms, where God's sovereign will is done without question by the angels who exist to serve him. This is why we pray as Jesus taught us, "Thy will be done on earth, as it [already] is in heaven."

Another sense in which the kingdom of God can be seen is in the life of a follower of Jesus. Because we follow the King, we have joined the kingdom. Because we have submitted to the laws of the kingdom, we are accounted as its citizens—not citizens of the politically defined State of Israel or members of the Jewish people, but citizens of God's eternal kingdom. Just as the ancient prophecies describe, we are non-Jewish followers of the King of the Jews.

Paul uses the term "inherit the kingdom of God" to describe the reward of those who follow Jesus. When he uses this terminology, he is talking about being alive during the Messianic Age. It will be a privilege and an honor to be able to live during that time under the rulership of King Jesus. To be a citizen of that eternal kingdom is part of the eternal reward of the faithful.

Paul also warns his readers that certain kinds of people will not inherit the kingdom:

> Do you not know that the unrighteous will not inherit the kingdom of God? Do not be deceived: neither the sexually immoral, nor idolaters, nor adulterers, nor men who practice homosexuality, nor thieves, nor the greedy, nor drunkards, nor revilers, nor swindlers will inherit the kingdom of God. And such were some of you. But you were washed, you were sanctified, you were justified in the name of the Lord Jesus Christ and by the Spirit of our God. (1 Corinthians 6:9–11)

Paul lists several sins that disqualify an individual from being a part of God's kingdom. These are the same sins we discussed earlier that were commonly associated with idolatry in first-century Judaism. Just as we discussed in the last chapter, those members of the nations who live in sin are going to be condemned at the last judgment.

Paul then reminds his readers that they used to find themselves in that situation. They had been idolaters and had embraced a sinful lifestyle. They had been on the "highway to hell," so to speak. Both individually and corporately, they'd had no standing before God that would have had a positive impact on their eternal destiny.

However, "in the name of the Lord Jesus Christ," these individual Gentile believers in Jesus were "washed," "sanctified," and "justified." In other words, they were no longer sexually immoral, idolaters, and such. Instead, they had been made righteous.

So when we begin to follow Jesus and we make him our King and we obey his commandments, we become part of the kingdom of God. At that point we are "justified"; God declares that we are righteous and that we can continue to be part of his kingdom into eternity—because God's reign ultimately will last forever, and only those who submit to his reign can live forever with him.

Along with this justification, we are placed into a new category—the body of Christ, the *ekklesia*, the church. As N.T. Wright has argued for so many years, the fact that believers in Jesus are now considered righteous cannot be separated from the fact that they are made part of a new group with its own corporate identity.[33]

In fact, this corporate change—this shift in identity from a member of the idolatrous nations to a non-Jewish member of the body of Christ—is the basis for the other blessings the disciple of Jesus receives through Christ. The corporate identity "in Christ" is primary; the personal justification of the Christian is secondary. The personal aspects of the gospel derive from the corporate aspects. God desires to work primarily through the body of Christ and secondarily through the individual members of that body.

Seeing salvation in this way, in a corporate sense, switches around what evangelical theology has come to regard as cause and effect. Jesus' disciples are not allowed into God's family because they have been personally declared righteous; rather, they are personally declared righteous because of their membership in the body of Christ, an entity that is by definition righteous because Christ is righteous.

Perhaps nowhere is this clearer than in Ephesians 2:19–22, where Paul finishes contrasting the fate of the members of the idolatrous nations with the fate of non-Jewish believers in Jesus:

> So then you are no longer strangers and aliens, but you are fellow citizens with the saints and members of the household of God, built on the foundation of the apostles and prophets, Christ Jesus himself being the cornerstone, in whom the whole structure, being joined together, grows into a holy temple in the Lord. In him you also are being built together into a dwelling place for God by the Spirit.

The disciple of Jesus does not become a righteous island, an isolated example of Christ's righteousness. Rather, he joins a singular body made up of Jesus-following Jews and Gentiles that is *corporately* becoming a "dwelling place for God," a "holy temple." Our personal righteousness is only part of this larger story. The purpose of this righteousness is not, as N.T. Wright argues, to effect our personal salvation, but to bring about God's larger plan for the entire world.[34] Our personal eternal destiny is not an afterthought, but neither is it at the center of what God is doing in the world.

Consider what this means for our quest to answer the question, "who are the people of God?" We now have two different people groups to consider. The Jewish people have a corporate covenant relationship with God through the patriarch Abraham, through the Sinai covenant, and through the promised new covenant. God has promised to be their God and that they will be his people.

The church, the body of Christ, also has a corporate covenant relationship with God. "In Christ" we become part of a defined group that is being built into a "dwelling place for God by the Spirit." As members of this group, we are the benefactors of many of God's promises that were originally promised to the Jewish people. However, these promises don't need to be taken away from the Jewish people in order to be given to us. Rather, Jesus has extended the scope of these promises to include us.

So now we have three groups we need to be aware of as we read through the Bible. The first is the Jewish people. The second includes all other nations of the world. The third is the body of Christ. While the first two groups do not overlap, the body of Christ overlaps with both.

The new identity of those Gentiles who have joined the body of Christ is not always clearly defined. Are they still Gentiles—members of the pagan nations of the world—or are they something brand new and different?

The answer seems to be "both." In terms of their relationship with the Jewish people, they are still classified as Gentiles; Paul, in many of his letters, continues to refer to the disciples of Jesus he has raised up among the nations as Gentiles in the present tense. However, as we consider their identity as members of the nations, Jesus-believing non-Jews are sometimes contrasted with these nations as if they were no longer under that classification (Ephesians 4:17; 1 Peter 2:12, 4:3).

Yet this ambiguity does not keep us from developing a clear idea of our role in God's plan to save the world. We (non-Jewish Christians) are no longer idolaters. We are no longer estranged from God. Categorically speaking, the nations of the world have yet to follow us into this new life of service to the God of Abraham. We have changed, while they have not; we are not like them anymore. In that sense we are no longer Gentiles—we are no longer categorically condemned because of our participation in corporate sins such as idol worship.

However, because we are not Jewish, we still recognize and accept our heritage as those from among the nations who have been called to follow the King of the Jews. In that sense we are still Gentiles. Our inner transformation is very real, and our placement in a new group (the body of Christ) is equally real, but our *social identity* as members of whatever nation we live in has been preserved.[35]

Because of this preserved social identity, because we are still American or Korean or Canadian or German, we retain our social connections with our countrymen. Through these channels we can continue to spread the good news of Jesus Christ. We can raise up disciples without having to cross, as Paul and Peter did, difficult social barriers. Our dual identity as followers of Jesus and members of the nations puts us in a powerful position to expand the kingdom of heaven.

## Analogies

There are many analogies and terms used to describe the church in the New Testament. We are "children of God" (John 1:12; Romans 8:16; Philippians 2:15; 1 John 3:1). As God's children, we are "fellow heirs with Christ" (Romans 8:17), since he is likened to God's firstborn son. We are the "body of Christ" (1 Corinthians 12:27), the physical representation of Jesus in the world. We are "God's temple" (1 Corinthians 3:16), the dwelling place for his presence. We are sheep in God's pen (John 10:16). We are children of Abraham (Romans 4:16).[36]

The church has built a lot of doctrine on these terms. But I think it is important to realize that if we take these analogies too literally, they become mutually exclusive and even contradictory. How can we be joint heirs with Christ if we are the body of Christ? How can we be sheep in a pen and the temple of God at the same time?

These word-pictures are used to illustrate deeper truths. We are children of God in that we are brand-new creations (2 Corinthians 5:17), not born of the flesh but of the Spirit (John 1:12–13). We are fellow heirs with Christ because he has extended many of the covenant blessings of the Jewish people to his non-Jewish followers. We are called the temple of God because the Spirit of God lives within us. We are called sheep—I think—because we tend to go astray (Isaiah 53:6). And we are children of Abraham because we share his faith in the living God (Romans 4:12).

But we should not take these metaphors beyond their intended meaning. We cannot infer from the fact that we are called "fellow heirs with Christ" that we will inherit everything Christ possesses. We will not become gods or receive all authority in heaven and earth, nor do we become Jewish, nor are we obligated to the customs and laws that specifically apply only to the Jewish people. Nor can we infer from the fact that we are "children of Abraham" that we need to become circumcised, as the Abrahamic covenant requires. These are separate issues, all of which are addressed clearly and specifically in the book of Acts and in the Epistles of Paul.

However, when properly understood, these beautiful word-pictures should fill us with awe and gratitude toward the God who sent his beloved Son, Jesus, on a mission to bring salvation not only to his covenant people but to idolatrous and apostate Gentiles as well—at the cost of his own life.

## Disciples

When the apostles looked for an Old-Testament-informed category into which non-Jewish disciples of Jesus fell, they found it in the books of the Prophets, who foretold that many members of the nations would someday come to the Jewish people and learn about the God of Abraham.

As disciples of the King of the Jews, we Gentile believers are learning from a Jewish rabbi how to properly relate to and obey the God of all creation. In doing so, we fulfill these ancient prophecies.

But it is important to note that before any Gentiles joined the Jesus movement, Jesus had already ascended into heaven. So we cannot follow him in a physical sense, or learn from him in the same way that students have traditionally learned from their teachers. Even if we had been alive in Jesus' day, those of us who are not Jewish would not have been able to follow him; we explained in *Yeshua Matters* that our Master almost never associated with or ministered to Gentiles.

It is hard to be disciples when our teacher is not physically present. It is even harder for us Gentiles when we realize that Jesus only ever had Jewish disciples during his earthly ministry.

But before Jesus ascended, he gave his apostles an important job: "All authority in heaven and on earth has been given to me. Go therefore and make disciples of all nations, baptizing them in the name of the Father and of the Son and of the Holy Spirit, teaching them to observe all that I have commanded you" (Matthew 28:18–20).

Since the days of William Carey, Christians have taken this passage as a mandate to spread the good news of Jesus across the globe and to raise up disciples of Jesus from all nations. I do not think this is wrong; I think the church must continue the work that the apostles started.

However, I also believe that the apostles had a key tool in their arsenal that we do not have: the authority of adjudication.

We find this tool referenced in Matthew 18:18, when Jesus told his disciples, "Whatever you bind on earth shall be bound in heaven, and whatever you loose on earth shall be loosed in heaven."

"Binding" and "loosing" are technical terms in Judaism. "Binding" refers to prohibiting or limiting an activity. "Loosing" has the opposite meaning; it refers to permitting an activity.

In other words, Jesus gave the apostles the command to go and make disciples of the nations—of people of all different nationalities and walks of life. As they did so, they were empowered to decide what discipleship looked like for non-Jews through forbidding or permitting certain activities.

The apostles, including Paul, had the authority to make binding pronouncements about how non-Jewish disciples of Jesus were supposed to live. When questions came up as to how a Gentile follower of Jesus should behave in a certain situation, because these disciples were in a new category, new decisions had to be made. New precedents had to be set. Jesus delegated this task to his apostles.

Roman Catholics believe that the power to adjudicate was passed on by the original apostles to their successors, a process that continues today. The adjudicating body of Roman Catholicism is called the apostolic college, and its head and representative is the bishop of Rome (at the time of this writing, Pope Francis). Catholics believe that the apostolic college has the same adjudicating authority the apostles had; this is how the concept of the Magisterium is justified in Catholic theology.

Protestants, however, do not have any authoritative person or group of people to make these kinds of decisions. I do not personally believe that the Roman Catholic apostolic college has apostolic authority, although I do not begrudge Catholics their decision to place themselves under its authority—that is their prerogative.

But this leaves us with a pressing question: to whom do we look for guidance when we aren't sure what Jesus would want us to do? The Jewish community has rabbis; the Catholic community has bishops. Whom do we have if we do not fall into either of those groups?

I think we have to try to answer, as best we can, how the apostles would have adjudicated any given issue, based on what they wrote down, as recorded in the New Testament. The apostles' intentions may also be reflected in another first-century document called the *Didache* (its full title would be translated something like "The Teachings of the Twelve Apostles for the Nations"). While the *Didache* is not part of the Bible, it is the oldest surviving Christian document besides the Bible. In fact, it was written earlier than some of the books in the Bible. It contains many specific directions for Gentile disciples of Jesus and claims to have its origins in the apostolic community.

You may not believe the *Didache* is a reliable source. After all, it was not canonized by the early church. But either way, when we encounter situations that the Scriptures don't speak to directly, we need to find out how the apostles would have decided any given issue. If we want to come up with the right answer, we need to understand what the apostles have written down—but to understand their writings, we need to understand their frame of reference, their time, their culture, their values. We need to understand first-century Judaism. And most Christians have never studied Judaism, ancient or modern.

So I propose a radical idea: interfaith dialogue.

Okay, maybe it isn't so radical.

But the Old Testament prophecies state that Gentiles will come to Jerusalem and learn about the God of Abraham from the Jewish people.

Christians have been around for two thousand years, but the Jewish people have been in covenant with God for twice that long. I think maybe they have some things figured out.

I don't think that Judaism is right about everything. In fact, many scholars have recognized that as Christianity grew and developed, Judaism changed in order to be less like Christianity. As Christianity distanced itself from Judaism over the first few centuries CE, Judaism in turn distanced itself from Christianity. Some things were changed, some added, some lost—on both sides.[37] Therefore, to study modern Judaism is not exactly to study the religion of the apostles.

But to try to piece together where we came from, what our movement was like in the beginning, and what the apostles would tell us now if they were alive among us, I think we need to be students of Judaism. We need to learn from the Jewish people. Even if we don't agree with them, we should hear them out and listen to what they have to say.

I know that people will criticize me for this. And I know that interfaith dialogue can be prickly and even dangerous. Many followers of Jesus have become so enamored with modern Judaism that they have begun to believe some of the ideas that Judaism developed specifically to counter Christian claims. They have adopted an extreme position on the unity of God, a position that doesn't allow for the existence of what the Apostle John called the Word made flesh, Jesus Christ. They have abandoned the Messiah altogether; God forbid that anything similar should happen as the result of this book.

On the other hand, nowhere in the New Testament do we see an example of non-Jews teaching other non-Jews about the kingdom of heaven without any Jewish presence or authority. In fact, I could make a pretty persuasive argument that the early church was a single, multi-campus megachurch, headquartered in Jerusalem and governed by the (Jewish) apostles.[38] Even if not, at the very least, we know that the apostles presided over the process of appointing elders for local churches (Titus 1:5), a system similar to the modern-day Catholic or Episcopal system of church government. The local church in the first century was under the apostles' authority; it was not autonomously governed.

So I'll make my proposal more specific. I believe that Christians should look toward Messianic (Jesus-believing) Judaism—and here I mean the formally defined community of Messianic Judaism[39]—for an idea of what the apostolic community might have been like. Messianic Jews inhabit a space where the Jewish people and the body of Christ—the two peoples of God we have discussed in this book—overlap. They belong to both groups, and consequently they have a unique role to play in God's plan.

I suppose that, more than interfaith dialogue, I am advocating interfaith dependency. Jesus-believing Jews have an important and prophetic role to help bring members of the nations under the wings of the Messiah. It is true that Messianic Judaism is still a young movement, and the Messianic Jewish community is still working out what it should look like to be a faithful Jewish follower of the Jewish Messiah. But the original template for the Jesus community had Jewish believers in Jesus—those who were already a part of what God had been doing, those who inhabited both peoples of God—taking a lead role in teaching and discipling the nations. To help the church rediscover this original template, I encourage non-Jewish Christians to support Messianic Jews as they grow into this prophetic and historic role.

I am not saying that Messianic Jews are the new apostles or that we aren't doing church right until Jewish people are in charge of everything. Neither I nor the leaders of the Messianic Jewish movement would advocate such a stance. But I do think that, more than anyone else, Messianic Jews have a biblically ordained role and calling to show the rest of us what the early church would have been like and to help us understand where the apostles were coming from by connecting us to the Jewish community, the original people of God, the recipients of the Torah.

By taking on this role, Messianic Judaism can become a vital bridge connecting us to our roots, to our past. I am sure that Messianic Jewish leaders would be happy to serve in this capacity if we asked them to.

# Israel

*Thus says the LORD: "The people who survived
the sword found grace in the wilderness; when
Israel sought for rest, the LORD appeared to
him from far away. I have loved you with an
everlasting love; therefore I have continued my
faithfulness to you."*

— *Jeremiah 31:2–3*

Remember Jacob, Abraham's grandson to whom the covenant blessings were passed? In Genesis 32 Moses recorded that Jacob wrestled a mysterious man—probably an angel or a representation of God himself. When Jacob won the wrestling match, God gave Jacob a new name: Israel. The one who wrestles with God—and prevails.

From that point on, Israel is the central focus of the biblical narrative. However, the name is not always used in the same way. If we were to look at each and every one of the thousands of uses of the word "Israel" in the Bible, we would find that each use falls into one of the following categories:

1. "Israel" can refer to Jacob, whose name was changed to Israel.

2. "Israel" can refer to Jacob's descendants, along with proselytes—in other words, to the Jewish people.

3. "Israel" can refer to the land of Israel, which took that name after the Israelites conquered it.

4. "Israel" can refer to the unified nation-state of Israel under the great kings of Israel, David and Solomon. In this way it can also refer to a future united kingdom of Israel, the eschatological kingdom over which the Messiah will reign.

5. "Israel" can refer to the northern kingdom of Israel, idiomatically called Ephraim or Samaria, which came into existence when the nation-state of Israel split in half under the reign of Solomon's son Rehoboam.

The word "Israel" is never used in the Bible to describe anything outside these five categories.[40] It is never used to describe the church as such; the idea that the church is "true spiritual Israel" comes from the early church fathers. These men believed that God had passed over the Jewish people and that all the blessings and promises God had given to them were now the property of the church. In patristic theology, the church had to take over the identity of "Israel" to inherit Israel's promises. This theological idea was created for one practical reason—to justify pushing the Jewish people aside to make room for the church to take their place.[41]

But this conclusion was incorrect. The church is not Israel. "Israel" is another term for the Jewish people.

Yet there is a sense in which the church is *one with* Israel. Paul writes of this mystical union in Ephesians chapter 2:

> Remember that at one time you Gentiles in the flesh, called "the uncircumcision" by what is called the circumcision, which is made in the flesh by hands—remember that you were at that time separated from Christ, alienated from the commonwealth of Israel and strangers to the covenants of promise, having no hope and without God in the world. But now in Christ Jesus you who once were far off have been brought near by the blood of Christ. (Ephesians 2:11–13)

Gentiles, members of the nations of the world, were "alienated from the commonwealth of Israel." Now, however, "in Christ," we "have been brought near." Paul continues, "So then you are no longer strangers and aliens, but you are fellow citizens with the saints and members of the household of God" (Ephesians 2:19).

If we have now been "brought near" to Israel and are "fellow citizens" along with the Jewish people, how does that work? What does it mean?

## Commonwealth

As if it has not been said enough, Gentiles don't become Jewish when we enter the kingdom of heaven. Entire books of the Bible were written just to prove that one point.

But we do, in some way, become part of Israel—"fellow citizens," along with the rest of God's people, the Jewish people.

How can this be so if "Israel" is simply a synonym for "Jewish"?

Recall that the word "Israel" has five different meanings in the Bible. One of these meanings is the nation-state, the kingdom of Israel. Just as Israel is a country today, in ancient times Israel was a kingdom; just as people of many different nationalities can live in the same country, so many different nationalities can live together in one kingdom, under one king.

So how do we become part of Israel? When we become part of the kingdom of heaven and place ourselves under the authority of Jesus we also become part of what we might call the "commonwealth of Israel," which includes everyone who submits to the King of Israel. This commonwealth of Israel will someday become a political reality when the eschatological kingdom of Israel is restored under the kingship of Jesus Christ.

The Jewish people are already part of the commonwealth of Israel because of the eternal covenants God has made with them. But Gentiles who choose to place themselves under the authority of the King of the Jews are also added to the commonwealth of Israel.

In this sense the church can be seen as a "multinational extension of Israel."[42] In this capacity we carry a piece of the mission of Israel with us: to submit to the God of Israel and to show the world what that kind of life looks like.

So is the church Israel? No—at least, there is not a one-to-one correlation between the terms "church" and "Israel." However, we do join *with* the nation of Israel and come alongside her as an extension of Israel to expand and realize the kingdom of heaven on earth.

# Reappraisal

In the past few chapters, I have tried to lay out definitions of the Jewish people, the nations, the church, and Israel. In these definitions, I have tried to remain faithful to what the Bible plainly teaches. I have not tried to articulate a theology of individual eternal destinies. Instead, I defined several people groups, attempting to remain faithful to a historically contextual reading of the Scriptures.

I have probably raised more questions than I have answered. Are all Jews automatically saved? If so, why? If not, why not? What about non-Jews?

And what does the eternal state look like? Do the categories of Jew and Gentile continue to exist after we are raised from the dead?

I do not want to try to answer these questions quite yet. Instead, I want to focus on one specific idea—the idea that the Jewish people have a unique and eternal covenant relationship with God—and explore what that idea means for Christians.

I believe that, in light of this information, since the Bible clearly teaches that the Jewish people have this status before God, we need to reappraise our identity as Christians.

For two thousand years we have answered the question, "who are we?" without stopping to remember that we are not the only people who have a relationship with God. To borrow an analogy from N.T. Wright, we have put the "church" puzzle together without taking all the pieces out of the box, and as a result, the picture we are working from is incomplete.

Our walk of faith, the way we practice Christianity, our priorities and actions in life, are determined by who we think we are and how we believe we relate to God and others. If we have some fundamentally flawed ideas about our identity as Christians, and if we have never considered who the people of God are in a broader sense (that is, in a sense that includes the Jewish people), then our life of faith, our religious practice, is also flawed.

How flawed? I can't speak to your individual situation, but I think that most Christians would change certain things about the way they "do" Christianity if they really stopped to think about who the Jewish people are and what their relationship with God is like.

In the next part of this book I want to explore exactly how things would and could change if Christians around the world recognized the unique role and calling of the Jewish people and affirmed that the covenants and promises God has made to them are still valid and in force.

*Part 2*

# Applications

K nowing that the church and the Jewish people are intimately related as peoples of the God of Abraham, we must ask, how does that relationship play out in real life? What should Jewish-Christian relations look like, and what is the role of non-Jewish believers in Jesus in that relationship?

# Standing with Israel

*I will establish my covenant between me and
you and your offspring after you throughout
their generations for an everlasting covenant, to
be God to you and to your offspring after you.
And I will give to you and to your offspring after
you the land of your sojournings, all the land of
Canaan, for an everlasting possession, and I will
be their God.*

— Genesis 17:7–8

For some readers this will be the most difficult chapter of this
book. Those of us who come from a background in dispensationalism, almost down to the last person, support the right of the
Jewish people to live in the land of Israel. Dispensationalists believe
that the land of Israel will always and forever be the possession of
the people of Israel, the Jewish people. In fact, when the Jewish
people officially established the modern State of Israel in 1948,
dispensationalists all over the world felt that their beliefs were
vindicated—that Bible prophecy was unfolding before their eyes.

However, many Christians reject the dispensationalist position
and do not believe that the Jewish people have an inherent right
to live in Israel. Many of them feel strongly that the modern State
of Israel is fundamentally misguided, or even bad, wrong, and evil.

The current conflict in the Middle East is, to be sure, one of the
defining issues of our time. The stand that America has taken as an

ally of the State of Israel and the level of involvement that America has had in the Middle East have caused many of the peoples and nations of that area to resent America. In fact, in 2002 the infamous terrorist Osama bin Laden wrote a letter in which he stated that the terrorist attacks of September 11, 2001, were carried out in part as a reaction to America's support of Israel.

In addition, many pundits, political commentators, and activists believe that Israel is an apartheid state in which Jews are given the royal treatment while the Arab minority is heavily discriminated against. The Palestinians are seen as a modern-day David, fighting the Israeli Goliath for control of the only homeland they have ever known. The Jewish people are portrayed as imperialists, blithely colonizing land they have no right to settle in.

Christians are divided on this issue. Prominent Christian teachers such as John Piper and Gary Burge have publicly declared that the Jewish people have no right to the land of Israel because they have not fulfilled the provisions of the Law of Moses—specifically, the commandment to believe in Jesus, the prophet who is like Moses, which we discussed in an earlier chapter. Others, such as John Hagee and Pat Robertson, vocally support the State of Israel because they believe that the promise of the land is part of God's eternal covenant with Abraham.

There may be no new revelations in this chapter. However, I do think it is worth revisiting the issue armed with a solid idea of who the Jewish people are, what their relationship with God is, and what the church is.

But first we need to understand both sides of the argument. And that, I believe, is the truly difficult part.

## Apartheid

Apartheid was the system of institutionalized racial discrimination in post–World War II South Africa. The struggle of black South Africans to gain equal rights and representation alongside the Afrikaner minority was a major political issue for decades. Apartheid finally ended in the 1990s, but its legacy lives on. Apartheid is a byword, a bad word, a nasty word that represents the ugliness of racism, hate, selfishness, and oppression.

Israel has been called an apartheid state. Ever since the foundation of the modern State of Israel, Jewish people in Israel have had a different legal status than that of any other people group. Under the Law of Return, passed soon after Israel's establishment, Jewish people can immigrate to Israel and become citizens with little or no difficulty. People of other nationalities may find it much more difficult to immigrate to Israel, and are certainly not guaranteed the right to do so.

There are other laws in Israel that treat non-Jews differently from Jews. For example, an Arab or Palestinian who owned land in Israel during the 1948 War for Independence—in which the State of Israel, newly formed by the United Nations Partition Plan, was immediately attacked by the surrounding nations—but who fled the country or fought against Israel during the war cannot recover ownership of his land today. This law is designed to make it easier for Jewish people to recover and own land, because after all, the goal in establishing the State of Israel was to create a homeland for the Jewish people.

For someone who believes that the Jewish people should have a homeland of their own, these kinds of laws make sense. After all, it should be easy for Jewish people to return to and possess the land God promised them. Even from a secular Jewish perspective, it makes sense that the Jewish people should have a nation of their own, a safe place they can call home—especially considering how badly Jewish people have been treated in other countries for the past two thousand years. It is impossible to argue that Israel isn't the natural location for such a Jewish state—as one secular talk-show host put it, "The Jews are the indigenous people of that area."

However, from the perspective of an outsider who is not Jewish and does not believe that the Jewish people have any kind of God-given right to the land of Israel, to allow Jewish people special legal rights is just another form of racism. It is inequality, enshrined in law and enforced by a civil justice system. Even some Jews feel this way.

To have a land that is designated for one nationality runs counter to modern progressive sensibilities. To say that Israel is for the Jews sounds perfectly fine to a dispensationalist, but the same dispensationalist might react more negatively to a statement like

"America is for the Americans"—or, to hit a more sensitive nerve, "Germany is for the Germans."

The twentieth century saw ethnic nationalism taken to the extreme in Germany before and during World War II. Consequently, in the post-war world, any sort of ethnic nationalism is automatically compared to Nazi Germany. But it is especially ironic, in the worst sort of way, that many of Israel's enemies compare Jewish nationalism to German National Socialism (Nazism), since the State of Israel was founded explicitly for the Jewish people partly because of the horrific atrocities of the Holocaust.

The State of Israel has never committed any sort of atrocity on the scale of the Holocaust. So this comparison is not warranted at all. But this accusation, as repulsive as it is to me personally, has found an audience. Even some Christians believe it.

To reiterate, I do not believe that there is any valid comparison between apartheid or Nazi ideology and the modern State of Israel. I personally believe that these accusations are ultimately rooted in anti-Semitism and were originally formulated by anti-Semites. It seems to me that people who accuse Israel of being an apartheid state are either looking for an excuse to hate the Jewish people or have been fooled into thinking that these accusations are not anti-Semitic in origin.

Even if we disagree with this viewpoint, however, we need to understand the current political reality if we are going to take a stand on either side of this issue. There is no point in arguing with people if we don't understand their position. After World War II, after the civil rights movement, after apartheid, the world is more sensitive than ever to anything that smacks of racial discrimination. Everyone wants to join a cause, everyone wants to be part of a movement, and everyone wants to feel as if they are standing with the oppressed.

We see regular reports in the news media of Israeli retaliation against Palestinians in the West Bank and Gaza Strip, pictures of crying Palestinian children, and stories of discrimination against Arabs. We assume as well that the Jewish people are safe and happy, and that they are not being oppressed by their own government— that despite their long and torturous struggle for life throughout the centuries, at the moment the Jewish people enjoy the freedom to govern themselves and to live in relative peace and safety.

With all this information in front of us, it is not hard for some to believe that minorities in Israel are oppressed. Our memories are short: the Jewish people, who less than a century ago were one of the most oppressed people groups on the planet (and had been such for nearly two thousand years), are now called oppressors—now that they finally have a home of their own. As a result, many Christians have taken up the Palestinian cause.

## Brothers

To add another layer of complexity, many Palestinians, Lebanese, and members of other non-Jewish populations in and around Israel are Christians. These Christians are, for the most part, members of the ancient liturgical churches that have persisted in the area since the time of Christ. Some of their liturgy is in Aramaic, the language Jesus probably spoke. Their history is a long and venerable one, and their continued existence is inarguably significant to the broader Christian community.

Most Palestinian Christians who lived in Israel before 1948 are now gone. While Palestinian Christians have not been singled out by Israelis for any kind of persecution, the emigration of Palestinians has contributed to a percentage decline of Christianity in Israel, since most Israeli Christians are Arabs.

In addition, Jews who believe in Jesus have historically not been allowed to immigrate to Israel under the Law of Return. While some have—and in recent days this situation has undergone some interesting changes in favor of Messianic Jews—for most of Israel's history it has been far more difficult for a Jewish believer in Jesus to immigrate to Israel than for a Jew practicing Judaism or even for a secular Jew. This difficulty is not as unreasonable as it sounds; Jews who convert to Christianity are not accounted as part of the Jewish community by the laws of traditional Judaism—a stance informed by the reality that most Jews who have become believers in Jesus throughout history have been required by the church to give up their Jewish identity. (The existence of a community of Jesus-believing Jews has become an issue only within the last century, with the emergence of Messianic Judaism as a worldwide movement.)

Finally, Lebanon, one of the nations with which Israel has gone to war (in order to retaliate against attacks by terrorist groups based in Lebanon), has a large Christian population. The church in Lebanon is ancient and has had a continuing presence there probably since the time of Christ. While Israel did not single out Christians, and instead rooted out terrorist cells that had made their home in Lebanon, certainly many Christians were harmed in some way as a result of the war—they were "collateral damage," so to speak. And depending on one's perspective, Israel, because they crossed over the border into Lebanon, could be seen as the aggressor.

For these reasons, some Christians feel that the State of Israel has had a harmful effect on Christians in the Middle East or that Christians are unfairly treated in Israel.

As a result, when these Christians take a side in the Israeli-Palestinian conflict, they choose to side against the Israelis. They feel that by doing so they are standing with their brothers and sisters in Christ who live in Israel or the surrounding territories.

## Apocalypse

Of course, not all Christians feel this way. Many Christians support Israel.

I am proud to count myself among them. While I am sensitive to the plight of the Palestinians, I know better than to believe that the Israeli government is to blame for their seemingly hopeless situation. Israeli armed forces must continue to maintain a strong presence in "occupied" territories because when that presence is removed, state-sponsored terrorist cells immediately fill the power vacuum.

The current (at the time of this writing, which was in the summer of 2014) conflict in Gaza is a prime example. As a show of good faith toward the Palestinians and toward the international community, Israel completely pulled out of the Gaza Strip in 2005; Gaza became a Jew-free zone. The Palestinian residents of Gaza could have taken that opportunity to establish a peaceful government and to begin the process of building a better life for themselves. The State of Israel provided material support to Gaza for precisely that purpose—building materials are regularly delivered to Gaza on Israel's dime.

But that opportunity for peace was passed by. Instead, the terrorist organization Hamas came to power within the space of a year. Hamas has dedicated itself to the total destruction of the State of Israel. So instead of building schools and hospitals, Hamas has built underground tunnels in an attempt to infiltrate Israel with the stated purpose of killing as many Israeli civilians as possible.

The states that sponsor terrorist groups like Hamas have done nothing to help the Palestinians, despite their ethnic and religious ties, because these terrorist groups have found it advantageous to have civilian centers from which to operate. Despite the dramatic toll this has taken on the Palestinian community, these terrorist cells believe so strongly in the eradication of Israel that they are willing to pay any price.

Furthermore, though ethnic nationalism has proven to be a dangerous and even murderous ideology in the wrong hands, the Jewish people are not an ethnic group, and Zionism is not ethnic nationalism. We explained earlier that Jewishness has national, ethnic, and religious dimensions, but the Jewish people are best described as a nation. With the establishment of the State of Israel, that nation has finally returned to its land. To accuse the Israeli government of racial discrimination is to fundamentally misunderstand what it means to be Jewish, to be part of the nation of Israel.

However, though I join with dispensationalists in supporting Israel, I must also offer a gentle rebuke; Christian support of Israel sometimes has a darker side to it.

While many Christians—and assumedly all dispensationalists—sincerely love and support the Jewish people, dispensationalist theology is not always about love and support for its own sake. Dispensationalists believe that Israel will be the location of a cataclysmic end-time battle called Armageddon. In this battle Israel will fight against the enemies that surround her. In the end she will prevail, with God's help. Dispensationalists look to Israel's supernatural victory in this end-time war as a herald of the second coming of Christ.

There has been a great deal of conflict leading up to this great final battle. Terrorist attacks and periodic all-out war in the Middle East have been regular occurrences ever since Israel was established in 1948. As the situation intensifies, I often see dispensationalists on the edge of their seats, waiting for the next explosion, the next attack, the next war. It seems as if they are waiting for the situation to escalate, because when the final breaking point comes, they believe that Jesus' return will be right around the corner.

This morbid fascination with conflict is surely not in the heart of every dispensationalist. I don't believe that dispensationalists are actually warmongers. But a quick glance at dispensationalist literature makes it easy to believe that they are. In newsletters, television shows, and books, dispensationalist teachers continually highlight the tension and conflict in the Middle East and constantly reassure their followers that this conflict is paving the way for the Messiah's return.

Try to look at this phenomenon from a Jewish person's point of view. Many of the casualties in this conflict are Jewish people. Someone who has lost a father, a brother, a sister in the repeated conflicts between Israel and her neighbors does not want to hear that Jesus is about to return as a result. When my Jewish friends in Israel relate that a friend or relative has been killed by terrorists, there is no joyful anticipation in their voices. There is only sorrow and the pain of loss. How do you think these Jewish people feel when they see Christians sitting on the sidelines with *anticipation*, waiting for something big to happen?

When Jewish people see Christians respond in this way, it certainly does not give them a pleasant feeling about Christ or his followers. The Jewish people want peace, not war. Like anyone else, they want to feel safe at night. They want to see an end to the violence—a peaceful end, not a nightmarish apocalypse.

I realize that the book of Revelation prophesies a cataclysmic end-time war in Israel. This same war is also prophesied in the Old Testament, the Jewish Bible. So the Jewish people know about these prophecies. Many religious Jews, like dispensationalists, believe that conflicts and tragedies will unfold before the Messianic Age begins; these are referred to as the birth pangs of the Messiah.

However, one of the most well-known teachings of Judaism is that one should love peace and pursue it.[43] We can surely take a lesson from this teaching. We should "pray for the peace of Jerusalem" (Psalm 122:6) and not get excited over increasing tension and conflict in the Middle East.

I think many dispensationalists and end-time prophecy buffs could use a reminder from one of the prophets of ancient Israel who caught a prophetic glimpse of the final day:

> Woe to you who desire the day of the LORD! Why would you have the day of the LORD? It is darkness, and not light, as if a man fled from a lion, and a bear met him, or went into the house and leaned his hand against the wall, and a serpent bit him. Is not the day of the LORD darkness, and not light, and gloom with no brightness in it? (Amos 5:18–20)

Do we desire the day of the LORD? Do we look with expectation not to the coming kingdom, but to the bloodbath that will precede it? Or, like the prophet Amos, do we dread the coming judgment? Do we weep for the outpouring of God's wrath?

Pray for the peace of Jerusalem.

# Gift

All that being said, I do think there is a rational stance that Christians can and should take in relation to the current situation in the Middle East.

First of all, we must realize that the promises God made to the Jewish people were made thousands of years before the modern ideas of nationalism, racism, and discrimination came to the forefront of the world's consciousness. It would be accurate to say that when the Jewish people conquered the land of Canaan around 3,500 years ago, it was a simpler time.

In ancient times each people group had its own gods and its own land. If another people group came in and conquered a certain nation, the conquering people's god was assumed to be stronger than the god of the nation that had been conquered.

In this ancient religious climate, God showed that he was more powerful than all the gods of Egypt by visiting ten terrible plagues on the Egyptian people. Then, when the children of Israel conquered the land of Canaan, God again demonstrated that he was stronger than all the gods of the Philistines and the other Canaanite peoples by granting Israel victory in battle after battle—often through great supernatural acts.

God's stated reason for allowing the Canaanites to be annihilated was that they had embraced a lifestyle so repugnant, so sickening, that there was no hope for their repentance and restoration. Even the Assyrian capital of Nineveh was given a chance to repent through the prophet Jonah, and the Assyrians were known for flaying conquered peoples and nailing their skins to the victims' city walls. So we can only imagine how bad it was in Canaan.

At any rate, when Israel conquered the land, the surrounding nations would have understood that the land belonged to the children of Israel by right of conquest. Their God had demonstrated his superiority over the gods that had previously ruled over the land of Canaan. There is no use trying to apply modern ideas of war and conflict to this ancient scenario. This was simply the way things were done back then.

However, there is also no use applying ancient standards of conflict and warfare to the modern State of Israel. The Palestinian refugees are not Philistines or Canaanites. God has not ordered their destruction. This situation must be handled in a totally different way.

It is possible and even probable that in trying to handle the Palestinian situation, the State of Israel will make mistakes. Israel is not operating under a theocratic monarchy. Jesus is not sitting on the throne in Jerusalem. The modern government of Israel is mostly secular and not religious—and certainly not consciously aligned with the teachings of the Messiah King, either in its secular or religious parties. So even a person who supports the right of the Jewish people to live in the land of Israel does not have to support every action of the secular government of Israel. As in any human government, its members will sometimes make poor decisions.

When I asked a few friends and some friends of friends to read through the first draft of this book, it was pointed out to me that the decisions of the Israeli government are magnified and criticized beyond those of any other government. The Israelis are put under a microscope, so to speak, and every potential error, every unfortunate casualty, every decision that could possibly be interpreted in a negative light is loudly reprimanded. I think this is true. In a sense we are dealing with the problem of propaganda. Most, if not all, readers of this book live in a nation that has at some point in time done evil things to retain power. The writer finds himself in the same predicament. There is a kernel of truth, however small, in the adage that "behind every great fortune lies a great crime."[44] However, we generally refuse to see or admit these morally questionable actions—historical or current—because it is incredibly difficult to live day after day with the knowledge that our comfortable lives are, at least to some degree, built on someone else's misfortune.

Israel's enemies, the nations that surround her, are conspicuous in their reliance on this self-justification process. The atrocities many of these governments have committed, both toward Jewish people and toward Palestinian refugees, are uncountable. Most of them will never be revealed or seriously considered on a national or worldwide scale. While there are exceptions (for example, American political conservatives are highly critical of the undemocratic governments of many Middle Eastern nations), the people of the world are, for the most part, willing to look the other way.

The same holds true for major media outlets. I am currently writing in the summer of 2014, and for the better part of a year, the Islamic State (IS, also known as ISIS or ISIL) has been recruiting child soldiers to murder civilians—many of them Christians—throughout Iraq and Syria. IS continues to fight its way west toward Israel, toppling regional governments and instituting strict Islamic law along the way. Major international newswires have downplayed these events, choosing instead to hold Israeli operations on Gaza under a microscope for the past several months, despite the fact that the Gaza conflict has occasioned far fewer casualties. The world simply doesn't hold Hamas, IS, or the governments of other countries in the Middle East to the same standard to which it holds Israel.

I don't know how I feel about this. Israel was given the Torah. She was told that she would forever be living in a fishbowl, that the nations of the world would be watching her to see if this people, which claimed to be the unique people of a unique God, had really adopted an inspired way of life. Because Israel bears God's name, the nations of the world judge God by the actions of Israel. So while I do think it is hypocritical to focus on Israel's supposed mistakes while glossing over the atrocities of the nations surrounding Israel,

I also believe that Israel is unavoidably in the spotlight because of her prophetic role and calling.

But even if we decide to disagree with some action of the Israeli government, our disagreements are a separate issue from the right of the Jewish people to live in their ancient homeland, promised by God through an eternal covenant. It is possible to support the Jewish people in Israel and at the same time to take issue with what we might judge to be a misguided action or policy of the Israeli government. We can love and support the Jewish people in Israel and still disagree with how the Israeli government handles certain situations. We must remember that the final redemption of the Jewish people is still coming. Their national regathering is a key step in that process, but it is not the final step. Until the redemption is complete, the nation of Israel will not be perfect.

However, before we even come to a position of criticizing the Israeli government, we must be sure we have heard both sides of the story. Most of us have never been on both sides of the fence between Gaza and Israel. We have not known the difficulty of life in Gaza, nor have we known the terror of hearing air raid sirens in Israel and knowing that we, our friends, and our family are in mortal danger. We have heard many things, but most of us have not seen both sides of the situation firsthand. So to open our mouths and begin to criticize the Israeli government is often to speak from a position of ignorance.

I believe that it is often better *not* to take a stand on highly charged incidents when we don't have all the information. Rather, we can stand on certain principles that we know to be true from the Scripture:

1. The Jewish people have been given the land of Israel as an eternal inheritance (Genesis 17:7–8).

2. It is the responsibility of the Jewish people not to oppress other nationalities and ethnic groups that live in their land: "You shall not oppress a sojourner" (Exodus 23:9).

3. Even in the harshest conflict, peace must be offered before violence is considered: "When you draw near to a city to fight against it, offer terms of peace to it" (Deuteronomy 20:10).

4. People and nations have every right to defend themselves against violent aggression. Jewish law, based on the property rights and personal rights outlined in the Torah, states that one whose life is in danger may kill the source of the threat.[45]

We can hold the actions of both Israel and her enemies to these basic principles. For example, terrorists do not attempt to negotiate peace before bombing Israeli civilians. These acts of violent aggression against innocent bystanders are morally unacceptable.

However, the Israeli government must take seriously its responsibility not to oppress the sojourner. While appropriate measures must be taken for self-defense, it is dangerously easy to cross the line into harming or oppressing innocent people. We must be sensitive to the difficulty of negotiating that line and to the immense complexity of the situation, but at the same time, we must not send the message that "anything goes" when it comes to Israeli police actions. To do so would be to tell the Palestinians that we do not consider them human or care about their plight—and Jesus has commanded us to show love to all, even those we might consider our enemies.

Consider the rhetoric we often hear at prophecy conferences and on Christian television. Israel is seen as a homogenous Jewish nation, and Arabs and Palestinians are all lumped together as enemies of Israel and enemies of God. While we can and should condemn senseless acts of violence, we must never dehumanize an entire race or group of people. Peaceful Arabs make up a large minority of Israel's population; they are involved at every level of society, they are represented in the Knesset, they are actively engaged in institutions of higher learning, and many are vocally supportive of the nation of Israel and its government.

To reiterate, we often do not have enough information to come to a determination about any particular incident. We get one side or the other, or we get two sides of a story that look completely different. All we can safely do in such a situation, without the ability to investigate for ourselves, is remain true to our principles.[46]

# Battle

Consider for a moment the real nature of the conflict surrounding Israel. Strip away the politics and the human governments. Zoom out from individual incidents and look at the bigger picture. Remember the words of the Apostle Paul: "We do not wrestle against flesh and blood, but against the rulers, against the authorities, against the cosmic powers over this present darkness, against the spiritual forces of evil in the heavenly places" (Ephesians 6:12).

Paul speaks here of a battle that, at its heart, lies behind the scenes of our physical reality. In our time this battle has revealed itself as a campaign to discredit the God of Abraham.

God's promise to Abraham, sealed forever as a result of Abraham's faithfulness to leave his homeland, included permanent possession of the land of Israel. God has given the land of Israel to the Jewish people forever. To see this promise fulfilled in our time, to see the Jewish people return to their land after almost two thousand years, is incredible. It is, apart from events recorded in the Bible, unprecedented. It is miraculous. It testifies to the underlying reality that the God of Abraham keeps his promises. It is as if God has personally sent a message to the world: "See? I did exactly what I said I would do. How can you say that I am unfaithful? How can you say that I don't exist?"

Israel's existence is a finger in the eye of the secular, godless zeitgeist of the present day. It is an aberration in history, a clear sign that the God of Israel is still active and powerful. When we see the Middle East situation through this lens, the battle for Israel's existence is indeed a battle of the gods, just as it was when Joshua and his men crossed over the dry riverbed of the Jordan. The "spiritual forces of evil in heavenly places" would like nothing better than to make God a liar and to make the nation of Israel and the Jewish people disappear from the earth. But God says:

> If I have not established my covenant with day and night and the fixed order of heaven and earth, then I will reject the offspring of Jacob and David my servant and will not choose one of his offspring to rule over the offspring of Abraham, Isaac, and Jacob. For I will restore their fortunes and will have mercy on them. (Jeremiah 33:25–26)

As Gentiles who have joined themselves to the God of Israel, we play a critical role in this spiritual battle, in the fight for the redemption of the world. Part of that role is to come alongside the Jewish people and support them. As such, we should never find ourselves in the position of denying Israel's right to exist or denying Israel's right to defend against violent attacks directed at innocent people. We should never find ourselves in a position in which we are harming innocent Jewish people and destroying their livelihood by boycotting Israeli goods. We are fundamentally allied with the Jewish people, and though we may at times disagree with our allies, we are still allies, permanently bound together by our shared relationship with the God of Abraham.

And we must always, always pray for peace.

# Remembering the Poor

*At present, however, I am going to Jerusalem bringing aid to the saints. For Macedonia and Achaia have been pleased to make some contribution for the poor among the saints at Jerusalem. For they were pleased to do it, and indeed they owe it to them. For if the Gentiles have come to share in their spiritual blessings, they ought also to be of service to them in material blessings.*

— *Romans 15:25–27*

One of the most frightening and most overlooked subjects in the Gospels is God's opinion of wealth and poverty. While we will not go into detail here on Jesus' many teachings regarding money and possessions, there is one in particular that relates closely to the church's relationship with the Jewish people.

Recall that, in the Bible, people generally fall into one of two categories: Jews or Gentiles. The Jewish people are God's covenant nation; the Gentiles are members of all the other nations of the world. When Jesus called out a group of followers, a third group was created—the body of Christ. This third group includes members from both other groups.

Knowing this, let's revisit a teaching of Jesus that, in my experience, we tend not to take very seriously. It is recorded in Matthew 25:31–46:

> When the Son of Man comes in his glory, and all the angels with him, then he will sit on his glorious throne. Before him will be gathered all the nations, and he will separate people one from another as a shepherd separates the sheep from the goats. And he will place the sheep on his right, but the goats on the left. Then the King will say to those on his right, "Come, you who are blessed by my Father, inherit the kingdom prepared for you from the foundation of the world. For I was hungry and you gave me food, I was thirsty and you gave me drink, I was a stranger and you welcomed me, I was naked and you clothed me, I was sick and you visited me, I was in prison and you came to me." Then the righteous will answer him, saying, "Lord, when did we see you hungry and feed you, or thirsty and give you drink? And when did we see you a stranger and welcome you, or naked and clothe you? And when did we see you sick or in prison and visit you?" And the King will answer them, "Truly, I say to you, as you did it to one of the least of these my brothers, you did it to me."
>
> Then he will say to those on his left, "Depart from me, you cursed, into the eternal fire prepared for the devil and his angels. For I was hungry and you gave me no food, I was thirsty and you gave me no drink, I was a stranger and you did not welcome me, naked and you did not clothe me, sick and in prison and you did not visit me." Then they also will answer, saying, "Lord, when did we see you hungry or thirsty or a stranger or naked or sick or in prison, and did not minister to you?" Then he will answer them, saying, "Truly, I say to you, as you did not do it to one of the least of these, you did not do it to me." And these will go away into eternal punishment, but the righteous into eternal life.

This is one of many of the teachings of Jesus that does not fit cleanly into Christian theology about salvation and judgment. Instead of dividing the world into people who believed in him and people who didn't, or into people who followed him and people who didn't, Jesus will divide them up based on their actions. Again, as we remarked when we went through Romans 2, this is a common Jewish theme regarding the final judgment.

However, if we read the parable closely, there are actually three groups of people mentioned. The sheep are those from among "all the nations"—remember, the term "nations" usually means non-Jewish nations—who have acted kindly toward the poor and disenfranchised. The goats are those from the nations who did not help or act kindly toward those in need. Finally, there is a third group: "my brothers."

Who are the brothers of Jesus? Since Jesus is a Jew, his brothers and sisters, in a physical sense, are the Jewish people; in a spiritual sense, his followers are also his brothers and sisters.[47]

This explanation of the parable makes sense from a Jewish perspective. All the nations are gathered before Jesus for judgment. The destiny of the Jewish people and the followers of Jesus is not the point of this parable; as the people of God, their relationship with God through the Messiah King determines their eternal destiny. This relationship, along with the covenants that define it, are not mentioned at all in this parable, because the nations of the world do not corporately have a covenant relationship with God. But the nations must be judged, and they are judged according to their actions.

Specifically, they are judged according to how they treated those who were in physical need.

Even more specifically, they are judged according to how they treated poverty-stricken Jews and Christians.

What about the eternal destiny of believers in Jesus? While I believe that those who follow Jesus have a secure eternal destiny, I also believe that "wisdom is justified by all her children" (Luke 7:35)—in other words, that a person's beliefs are borne out by his or her actions. What we *really* believe will come alive in what we do.

The Lord's brother wrote, "What good is it, my brothers, if someone says he has faith but does not have works? Can that faith save him? If a brother or sister is poorly clothed and lacking in daily food, and one of you says to them, 'Go in peace, be warmed and filled,' without giving them the things needed for the body, what good is that? So also faith by itself, if it does not have works, is dead" (James 2:14–17).

The Apostle John wrote, "By this it is evident who are the children of God, and who are the children of the devil: whoever does not practice righteousness is not of God, nor is the one who does not love his brother" (1 John 3:10).

The brothers and sisters here, the children of God, are the followers of Jesus as well as the Jewish people.

It seems clear in all these passages that giving money, food, clothing, and other necessities to Christians, Jewish people, and presumably others who are in need *actually makes a difference in one's eternal destiny.*

Christians will be familiar with many passages that teach that all those who follow Jesus will have eternal life. Furthermore, the sheep-and-goat-judgment parable is not primarily about the destiny of Jews or of the followers of Jesus. But can we expect God to hold his people, who have in the Scriptures a clear revelation of God's will for their lives, to a lower standard than that to which he holds the nations of the world?

Jesus teaches that those among the nations who neglect the poor will not have eternal life. What does that say about our responsibility as his disciples to care for the poor? Do we think that we will be exempt from this responsibility because we are "in Christ?" Do we think that our affiliation with Jesus will cause him to lower the bar for our behavior, so that what is required of us is even less than what he requires of everyone else?

Consider this parable, which appears in Matthew shortly before the story of the sheep and the goats:

> Who then is the faithful and wise servant, whom his master has set over his household, to give them their food at the proper time? Blessed is that servant whom his master will find so doing when he comes. Truly, I say to you, he will set him over all his possessions. But if that wicked servant says to himself, "My master is delayed," and begins to beat his fellow servants and eats and drinks with drunkards, the master of that servant will come on

a day when he does not expect him and at an hour he does not know and will cut him in pieces and put him with the hypocrites. In that place there will be weeping and gnashing of teeth. (Matthew 24:45–51)

Jesus calls those who claim to be his servants but who ignore his commandments hypocrites. They are false-faced pretenders. They do not inherit eternal life; rather, they are cast out.

In light of the strength and clarity of Jesus' teaching in this area, I would argue that we must accept the fact that the Bible has defined following Jesus in a certain way. To follow Jesus is, at least in part, to help the poor. We can't follow Jesus without helping the poor.

As we do this, our primary targets for charity must be other disciples of Jesus and the Jewish people.

While it is important to help everyone who is in need, consider what people would think of a movement that does not even take care of its own people.

I am not saying we should help our own in lieu of helping others; we need to do both. In fact, I believe that Jesus identifies with all those in every nation who are poor and disenfranchised, and I believe that at the sheep-and-goat judgment, those from among the nations who never encountered Jews or Christians will still be held to account for how they treated the poor among them. But as members of a community of faith, we must be especially aware of needs in that community—and in the Jewish community.

## Charities

It is difficult for most Christians to directly help Jewish people who are in need. Most of us do not have connections within the Jewish community who can tell us what the needs are or what we can do to help. The relationship between Jews and Christians in many areas is so strained that it might be difficult to build this kind of relationship. A Christian's offer to help is likely to be interpreted as the beginning of an attempt to convert Jews to Christianity, and it is likely to be rejected.

However, there are several charities that have spent years building ministries that successfully help Jewish people who are in need. Giving to a charity is not as personally rewarding as helping a person directly, but it can be just as effective in helping to make others' lives better.

Some of these charities are run by Christians who are successfully building bridges with the Jewish community. Messianic Jews have also established numerous charitable organizations that connect Jesus with his people Israel through acts of kindness and unconditional love. You may even decide that it is worthwhile to simply donate to Jewish charities. Whichever way you might choose, charities enable Christians to support poor and disenfranchised Jewish people without having to personally negotiate sensitive community boundaries.

There are at least two reasons why it is important for each of us to make a commitment in this area. First, it helps to repair the broken relationship between Christians and the Jewish people. If enough Christians give enough of their own money to better the lives of poverty-stricken Jews, the Jewish people will begin to understand that we genuinely care about them for who they are and not just because we see them as potential converts.

Restoring this relationship is vital. As part of a multinational extension of Israel, Christians share in the mission and calling of Israel. But that mission and calling are damaged when the relationship between the groups that are called is broken.

Second, we are commanded to give anyway. We are required to help the poor; it is part of what following Jesus is all about. In fact, the Bible speaks so strongly to this area that we are forced to conclude that anyone who does not help the poor will be judged unfavorably on the last day. It is hard to reach any other conclusion from Jesus' teachings on this subject.

## *Bridge*

Another way that Christians can help those who are poor in the Jewish community is to begin cultivating a relationship with a Messianic Jewish synagogue.[48] Messianic Jews have a strong identity as members of the Jewish people as well as a strong faith in Jesus Christ. Because of their unique position, they can be a bridge between the Christian and Jewish communities.

A local Messianic Jewish synagogue may have connections with the Jewish community in your area. They will know best how you can help with any needs they may have. They may even have a charitable arm set up already, just as many churches have food pantries and emergency funds. If not, they should still be able to give you good advice.

Building a relationship with a local Messianic Jewish synagogue is important in its own right. Messianic Judaism is one of the most important movements of our time. It is wonderful to see Jewish people embrace Jesus as their Messiah King while retaining their identity as covenant members of the children of Abraham. This is how the apostles defined the early Jesus movement—Gentiles coming alongside Jewish people to follow the King of the Jews.

For many hundreds of years, something very different happened. To follow Jesus, Jews had to leave behind their identity as Jews and join a Christian church. Rather than embracing their identity as a multinational extension of Israel along with the Jewish people, Christians abandoned the idea that the Jewish people were still in covenant with God.

One important idea that has to be reexamined as we rediscover the role and calling of the Jewish people has to do with this very issue. It is the idea that Jesus-believing Jews should renounce Judaism, become Christians, and join the institutional church. We will explore this in the next chapter.

# Guarding Jewish Identity

*Let each person lead the life that the Lord*
*has assigned to him, and to which God has*
*called him. This is my rule in all the churches.*
*Was anyone at the time of his call already*
*circumcised? Let him not seek to remove the*
*marks of circumcision.*

— 1 Corinthians 7:17–18

S ome might say that one of the great shortcomings or tragedies of Christian history has been our failure to reach the Jewish people with the gospel.

I don't think so at all.

In fact, we have reached millions and millions of Jewish people with the gospel. We have probably reached more Jewish people with the gospel than there are Jewish people alive today.

The problem is that once these Jewish people confessed their faith in Jesus, we didn't let them be Jewish anymore. We wanted them to become just like us.[49]

We had Bible verses for this: "He himself is our peace, who has made us [Jews and Gentiles] both one and has broken down in his flesh the dividing wall of hostility by abolishing the law of commandments expressed in ordinances, that he might create in himself one new man in place of the two" (Ephesians 2:14–15). Or how about Acts 15:11: "But we believe that we [Jews] will be saved through the grace of the Lord Jesus, just as they [Gentiles] will."

Or this one:

> For freedom Christ has set us free; stand firm therefore,
> and do not submit again to a yoke of slavery. Look: I, Paul,
> say to you that if you accept circumcision [proselyte
> conversion and the resulting Jewish life], Christ will be
> of no advantage to you. I testify again to every man who
> accepts circumcision that he is obligated to keep the
> whole law. You are severed from Christ, you who would
> be justified by the law; you have fallen away from grace.
> … For in Christ Jesus neither circumcision [Jewishness]
> nor uncircumcision [Gentile-ness] counts for anything,
> but only faith working through love. (Galatians 5:1–4, 6)

These verses make it sound as if Jewish people who want to
follow Jesus should get rid of the things that make them different
from other disciples of Jesus ("the law of commandments expressed
in ordinances") in order to be part of one new thing that God is cre-
ating—the church. Paul in Galatians even makes it sound as if living
a Jewish life—that is, being circumcised—will cause a person to be
considered as "severed from Christ" and "fallen away from grace."

Paul seems to have taught clearly that being Jewish or not Jewish
doesn't count for anything either way and that we shouldn't even
acknowledge that there is a difference: "There is neither Jew nor
Greek, there is neither slave nor free, there is no male and female,
for you are all one in Christ Jesus" (Galatians 3:28).

However, we need to reexamine these verses and this particular
issue in light of what we have learned about who the Jewish people
are and how their relationship with God is defined.

## Zealous

Before we jump into Paul, let's look further into the Acts narrative
that we touched on earlier in this book.

After the incident with Peter and Cornelius, the Jerusalem
Council was called. The Apostle Paul was there to tell the council
of all the miraculous things that God was doing in the lives of non-
Jews all over the known world.

After the council was finished, Paul hit the mission field several more times, revisiting churches that he had planted and going on to plant new ones. His last journey was a long one; he stayed at Ephesus for several years to make disciples and to teach and preach to whomever came through town.

When he returned from his third journey, Paul went to Jerusalem to see the rest of the apostles. They were happy to see him and to hear about all the things God was doing. However, a problem was developing:

> They said to him, "You see, brother, how many thousands there are among the Jews of those who have believed. They are all zealous for the law, and they have been told about you that you teach all the Jews who are among the Gentiles to forsake Moses, telling them not to circumcise their children or walk according to our customs." (Acts 21:20–21)

There are many things we can learn from this short passage.

First, James and the other apostles in Jerusalem headed up a very large church that had thousands of Jewish people in it, and these Jewish people, under the direction and authority of James and the apostles, were "zealous for the law." They obeyed the Law of Moses, just as Jesus had taught his disciples to do, and just as the disciples-turned-apostles had continued to teach the growing number of Jewish believers in Jesus to do after the Lord's ascension into heaven.

Second, word had gotten back to these Jews that Paul was teaching something completely different. They had heard that Paul was teaching Jews not to be zealous for the law—in fact, that he was teaching them to abandon the law completely and not to live a Jewish life anymore.

This does seem to be what Paul was saying in the verses we just read.

To the apostles, however, this interpretation of what Paul had said was a huge problem, because Jesus had taught them to continue following the Law of Moses.

If Paul was not on the same page with the apostles, we have a real dilemma on our hands; as we discussed in an earlier chapter, .

God gave the twelve apostles the authority to decide what a Jesus-following Gentile's life of faith looked like. If Paul claimed to have that same authority but disagreed with the apostles, then how can we make sense of the Bible? Who do we listen to? Paul? Or James, Peter, and the rest?

James had a plan to fix the problem. He assumed that Paul was being misinterpreted. So he told Paul to do one of the most Jewish things possible: complete a nazirite vow at the Temple—animal sacrifices and all—and pay for several other Jesus-believing Jews to do the same thing.

Paul went through with James's plan: "Then Paul took the men, and the next day he purified himself along with them and went into the temple, giving notice when the days of purification would be fulfilled and the offering presented for each one of them" (Acts 21:26).

Now perhaps Paul was tricking the other apostles to make them think that he agreed with them and that he was continuing to keep the Law of Moses as Jesus had taught his disciples to do. Maybe Paul wanted the apostles to think that he was still living a Jewish life while in reality he had abandoned that life.[50]

I don't know if I would want to follow a person like that or if I would do what he recommended in any situation.

Fortunately for me and for Paul, I think that it is more likely that we have misinterpreted Paul. I don't believe that Paul was tricking the apostles; rather, I am convinced that he continued to live a Jewish life, and that his instructions about not living a Jewish life were not for Jews at all, but for Gentiles.

## Rule

Paul understood the ramifications of what had happened at Cornelius' house perhaps better than anyone else alive. He really understood that in order for the church to be what it was supposed to be, Gentiles needed to remain Gentiles.

Paul was called to the mission of teaching Gentiles what it meant to follow Jesus. The other apostles recognized this calling and blessed his efforts to reach non-Jews for the kingdom of heaven (Galatians 2:7–10).

We must never forget that Paul's primary ministry was to the Gentiles: "I have written to you very boldly by way of reminder, because of the grace given me by God to be a minister of Christ Jesus to the Gentiles" (Romans 15:15–16).

So when he wrote, "I, Paul, say to you that if you accept circumcision [that is, formal proselytization to Judaism and the resulting Jewish lifestyle], Christ will be of no advantage to you" (Galatians 5:2), he was writing to Gentiles. As if we needed to say it again, Gentiles who join the body of Christ do not need to become Jewish.

Paul made this argument in many ways with many words. When he wrote, "There is neither Jew nor Greek, there is neither slave nor free, there is no male and female, for you are all one in Christ Jesus" (Galatians 3:28), he was talking about being part of the community of faith in Jesus.[51] All Jesus' disciples are accepted into the body of Christ. Because of that, there is no need for a Gentile believer in Jesus to become Jewish—he doesn't need to join that people of God, because he is already part of the people of God as defined within the body of Christ.

However, later in Galatians Paul reminded his readers that if they did convert to Judaism, they would have to live fully Jewish lives: "I testify again to every man who accepts circumcision [that is, becomes Jewish] that he is obligated to keep the whole law" (Galatians 5:3).

Probably in order to help clear up the confusion about what he was teaching in this area, Paul wrote to the Corinthians:

> Only let each person lead the life that the Lord has assigned to him, and to which God has called him. This is my rule in all the churches. Was anyone at the time of his call already circumcised? Let him not seek to remove the marks of circumcision. Was anyone at the time of his call uncircumcised? Let him not seek circumcision. For neither circumcision counts for anything nor uncircumcision, but keeping the commandments of God. Each one should remain in the condition in which he was called. (1 Corinthians 7:17–20)

Earlier in this book we touched on half of Paul's teaching here—that a Gentile who commits to become a disciple of Jesus should not become Jewish.

Here, though, we need to look at the other half: Paul teaches here that a Jewish person who commits to become a disciple of Jesus continues to be Jewish.

The phrase "marks of circumcision" refers to more than just the physical sign of circumcision. It refers to all of Jewish life—keeping the commandments of the Law of Moses (including those that are obligatory only upon Jewish people) and the traditions of Judaism.[52]

So Paul, along with the other apostles, taught that when a Jewish person decided to follow Jesus, he or she needed to continue to live a Jewish life. According to Paul, this was a rule that applied everywhere, in all the churches.[53]

## Preservation

How should this work today? And what can non-Jewish Christians do to make sure this rule is followed?

The essence of what needs to happen in Christian churches today could be summed up as the preservation of Jewish identity. Jewish people who decide to follow Jesus need to continue to identify as Jewish and need to pass that identity down to their children.

Traditionally, Jewish identity has been tied to several things: being part of the Jewish community, keeping Jewish laws and customs, and circumcising one's male children so that they can continue to carry that Jewish identity forward through time.

We simply don't allow for these things to happen in our churches today. If we are going to follow Paul's "rule in all the churches," we are going to have to change our churches.

This is another issue that highlights the need for local churches to partner with Messianic Jewish synagogues. Jewish people who come to faith in a Christian environment can be given an opportunity to join a Jewish community of believers in Jesus—that is, if churches are willing to prioritize the biblical role and calling of the Jewish people over the size of their own membership rolls.

In an ideal world, every church would respect Paul's "rule in all the churches" and make changes to allow Jewish worship practices and traditions to be followed within the church, so that a Jewish person could find his Jewish identity within the institutional church and not have to look elsewhere. In fact, in an ideal world, we would still be doing things the way the apostles did, and Christianity would look a lot more like first-century Judaism. I sometimes wonder how Jewish the church would look today if we had never forgotten Paul's rule, never forgotten that Jesus was Jewish, and never forgotten that the Jewish people continue to have a unique covenant relationship with God.

I am not optimistic enough to believe that the church will actually make these radical changes. But I do think that we can do the next best thing. I believe that churches should encourage their Jewish members and congregants to get involved with local Messianic Jewish synagogues. In a synagogue environment, they will be able to connect with other Jewish believers in Jesus and share the common bond of Jewish identity together. They can live out Jewish life in community and reinforce each other's shared sense of *Yiddishkeit*, of Jewishness.

By guarding Jewish identity in this way, we restore God's structure and design for the church—a body of Jews and Gentiles working together toward the kingdom of heaven, and not an undifferentiated mass of people who have forgotten God's eternal covenant with the Jewish people.

We cannot even imagine what kind of blessing it will be to see God's design for the church restored. As someone who has experienced a tiny glimpse of what this would be like in my relationships with Messianic Jewish synagogues, organizations, and leaders, I can say confidently that God has immense rewards laid up for those who take the plunge and begin to support and learn from Messianic Judaism.

# Repairing Jesus' Reputation

*Who has believed what he has heard from us?*
*And to whom has the arm of the LORD been*
*revealed? For he grew up before him like a young*
*plant, and like a root out of dry ground; he had*
*no form or majesty that we should look at him,*
*and no beauty that we should desire him.*

— Isaiah 53:1–2

*Joseph recognized his brothers, but they did not*
*recognize him.*

— Genesis 42:8

In *Yeshua Matters* we asked the question, "why don't Jews believe in Jesus?" I gave a theological answer: because God wanted to give non-Jews the opportunity to join God's family on equal ground with the Jewish people. Paul taught in Romans 11 that God allowed the Jewish people to stumble for just a moment so that Gentiles could have time to attach themselves to Jesus before the final judgment.

But there are other answers to the question of why Jews don't believe in Jesus. One, which we also discussed, is the fact that Jews today believe that Jesus abandoned Judaism—that he abandoned the Jewish people to start a new religion: Christianity.

Jews believe this because Christians have taught it. We taught for nearly two thousand years that Jesus and Judaism were incompatible. They couldn't exist together. Judaism found its end in Jesus; any Judaism that kept going after Jesus was illegitimate. Judaism existed only to prepare the way for Christianity.

It is no wonder that Jews have rejected this representation of Jesus. They know better than to think that their Messiah would abandon his people and dismantle everything that Moses and the prophets, with God's direction, built.

We have proposed a different idea here: that the Jewish people still continue to have a covenant relationship with God. That Jesus didn't come to start a new religion, but instead remained a practicing Jew. That he was faithful to the Law of Moses and that he taught other Jews to live the same way.

How does this impact our evangelistic witness to the Jewish people? I would answer, "Much in every way" (Romans 3:2).

## Conversos

Historically, Jewish people have been required to give up their Jewish identity in order to follow Jesus. The Jewish community as a whole has never bought into this notion, which is all the reason it needs to reject Christianity as a whole. The Jewish people's everlasting covenant with God, which they have by virtue of their kinship with Abraham, requires them to continue living Jewish lives (Genesis 17).

But some Jewish people have indeed become Christians. Sometimes these conversions have even been coerced or forced. One of the best-known examples is that of the *conversos*, Jews who converted to Christianity during the late Middle Ages because they were pressured to do so by the Christian monarchs of Spain and Portugal. Eventually, Jews who refused to comply were forced out of these countries altogether; they had to convert to Christianity or lose their livelihood.

Many of these converted Jews continued to practice Judaism in secret. They retained their identity as Jews and continued to have contact with other Jewish people. As you can imagine, their treatment at the hands of Spanish Christians has not been forgotten; their stories were passed down within the Jewish community.

The Jewish community today remembers the *conversos* and millions of other Jews who have suffered at the hands of Christians. They remember poverty-stricken Jewish children in London who were lured to Christian indoctrination with the promise of food and sustenance. They remember Christians offering to teach Jewish children Hebrew, only to find that these classes were designed solely to convert the children to Christianity.[54]

These Christians wanted the Jewish people to recognize Jesus as their Messiah, and that is a desire I share as well. But the way these conversions were accomplished was foolish and immoral, and we are still dealing with the resulting fallout.

The Jewish community sees Christianity as a religion that wants to completely wipe out Judaism and the Jewish way of life. We have created that picture in their national consciousness by the way we have treated them through the centuries.

Even worse, the Jewish community sees Jesus as the ultimate destroyer of Judaism; after all, why else would his followers try to wipe out Judaism? Jesus must have taught them to.

Our actions have created a huge barrier, a huge stumbling block, that is part of what keeps the corporate Jewish community from being able to see Jesus for who he really is. Even though we may not have personally taken part in any activity that has been harmful to the Jewish community, we still need to take responsibility for the job of restoring Jesus' reputation, a reputation which has been damaged by years of harmful conversion tactics practiced by well-meaning Christians.

## Evangelism

The realization of the harm that some Christian mission efforts have caused the Jewish people must have a direct impact on the future of these efforts. If you have read *Yeshua Matters*, you know how critical it is for Christians to portray Jesus accurately. Both in our theology and in our practice, we must reflect the Jewish Jesus; besides being the only historically accurate Jesus, he is the only Jesus the Jewish people as a whole will ever accept.

Until we get the Jewish Jesus right, until we develop the ability to communicate him in his full Jewish regalia, we must reevaluate our methods when it comes to actively evangelizing Jewish people.[55]

I am certainly not suggesting that if a non-Jesus-believing Jewish person comes into your church, you should turn them away. In fact, I would hope and pray that as a result of this book and others like it, Christians will be far better equipped to handle such a situation in a way that allows everyone involved to remain faithful to Jewish identity and to the role and calling of the Jewish people.

Nor am I suggesting that the Jewish people do not need Jesus. On the contrary, as we discussed in the first section of this book, the final redemption of the Jewish people hinges on their acceptance of Jesus' person and his message. While God will ultimately bring this about, we would be foolish to discount the efforts of Christian missionaries toward this goal.

Nor do I intend to personally deprecate those who have dedicated their lives to spreading the gospel among the Jewish people, or to detract from the joy of those who *have* been introduced to Jesus through Christian missionary efforts.

But we must reflect on the past to learn from it, and at times, we must be self-critical. If we never admit our mistakes, we will go on repeating them. So in that spirit I strongly encourage those Christians who have a burden for the salvation of the Jewish people to soberly consider the effect that their actions may have on future generations of Jewish people.

We tend to think of evangelism as a dragnet. Every time we drag the net, we catch a few more fish; a few more souls are saved. Just drag the net enough times, and we will eventually catch everyone.

But evangelism is nothing like that. Evangelism is a vital human-to-human interaction that echoes throughout the communities of everyone involved and becomes part of the cultural memory of entire people groups. Stories are told and retold of kindnesses shown by a stranger from a community other than one's own, and after enough time, two whole people groups may grow closer together through these kinds of positive experiences.

You may think that I am exaggerating. As an example of this principle in action, consider King Charles XIV John of Sweden. Charles was not Swedish at all; he was born a French national named Jean Bernadotte. Bernadotte was offered the monarchy in

Sweden in part because of his fair treatment of Swedish prisoners of war during the Napoleonic Wars. Stories of his kindness were repeated throughout Sweden, increasing his reputation and endearing him to the Swedish people.

On the other hand, just as a single act of kindness can reverberate through history, a single offensive act can also have lasting consequences. Stories are told and retold of harm done by someone from a community other than one's own, and as time passes, communities can and do drift apart.

Each and every interaction between a Christian and a non-Jesus-believing Jewish person has aftereffects that ripple throughout both communities. A careless word, an insensitive comment, or an unpleasant conversation can all serve to reinforce negative stereotypes about Jesus and about Christians within the Jewish community. A failed evangelism attempt is a problem far weightier than one soul being delayed on its journey toward Jesus. It can actually cause the further hardening of an entire community toward the person and message of Christ.

I'm not saying Christians should halt their efforts to show Jesus to the non-Jesus-believing Jewish community. And I'm sure I'm not telling missionaries something they don't already know. But again, as we reconsider how things need to change in light of the continuing relationship God has with the Jewish people, we must also reevaluate the message we send to that community.

For example, do we give lip service to the Torah solely in order to entice religious Jews to reconsider Christian claims? Or do we seriously uphold the Torah as the continuing standard for God's people?

Do we claim to believe that the Jews are God's "chosen people" but at the same time deny that people's essential covenant relationship with God in our soteriology and ecclesiology?

Do we encourage Jewish believers in Jesus to adopt Jewish practices and establish Messianic synagogues in order that they might truly reflect authentically Jewish lives of faith, or are these things only tools to convince religious Jews that Judaism and Jesus are somehow "compatible"—as if Christ and the movement that bears his name are not essentially Jewish in character?

Do we uphold Jesus-believing Jews as a healthy and normal expression of faith, as great in value as any other Christian expression—and indeed, as the *original* expression of Christianity? Or do we simply consider them evangelistic tools whose uniqueness as Jews is useful only as bait to draw others from the non-Jesus-believing Jewish community?

I understand that these questions are harsh. But until we deal with the reality they represent, our efforts to reach non-Jesus-believing Jewish people with the message of Jesus Christ will be fraught with unnecessary danger and difficulty, and will cause preventable harm to the Jewish community.

Because of our collective past, because of things other people have done, we must hold ourselves to a very high standard. We must be completely blameless so that no one will be able to use our mistakes as a reason to reject the gospel. Above all, we must be hyper-aware of how our engagement with the Jewish community reflects on the character of Jesus. We must consider every interaction with every person, especially with non-Jesus-believers, and *especially* with non-Jesus-believing Jews, as an opportunity and a responsibility to reflect our Master accurately. Let the weight of this responsibility keep us from repeating the mistakes of our past.

## *Resources*

The Messianic movement is still in its infancy. Compared to what one might find within Christianity or Judaism, there are not very many Messianic publishing companies. There are not many Messianic devotionals, study guides, or Bible helps. As a result, it is hard for Messianic Jews and Gentiles to show the world and specifically the non-Jesus-believing Jewish community who Jesus really was—a faithful Jew.

At some point I believe that the Messianic movement will become mainstream. I believe that the Jewish Jesus will not remain lost in the mist of history. I believe he will emerge clearly and challenge the status quo of our religious landscape, just as he challenged the status quo during his earthly ministry.

But for now, there is not a very large market for Messianic resources. Projects designed to help the Messianic community grow and mature take a long time to produce and a lot of effort to polish. It costs a lot of money to produce a book, and since there aren't very many people—yet—who understand how important these resources are, that investment is hard to recoup.

A Messianic Jewish synagogue will never be quite complete without a Messianic Jewish Siddur (prayer book). It will always be difficult to show religious Jews the quintessentially Jewish nature of the New Testament without accurate and beautifully produced translations of the Gospels and Epistles into Hebrew. The writings of early Messianic Jewish pioneers, many of whom witnessed to the Jewish community with strength and clarity in a culturally sensitive and appropriate way, will be lost to history unless they are translated and reprinted.

Commentaries on the Bible from a Messianic Jewish perspective, which open up the Jewish world of the text, have so far failed to fill the shelves of the pastors and teachers who could most benefit from them.

There also remain many unwritten books about the presence of Jesus, hints of the Messiah, all throughout Jewish literature from the past two thousand years. Not to mention books that teach Christians about Jesus and the early church and how their roots lie in Judaism. We are short of all these things.

However, there are people who would dedicate their lives to producing these kinds of resources if the finances were available.

There are many organizations seeking to accomplish this same mission: this book's publisher, her sister ministry Vine of David, the New School for Jewish Studies, and the Messianic Jewish Theological Institute are all staffed with Messianic Jews working hard to restore an authentic, truly Jewish picture of Jesus, and to help both Christians and Jews understand better who the rabbi from Nazareth was and what he taught. To support these organizations is to directly support the reparation of Jesus' reputation among his people.

## Repentance

The more Christians who come to the realization that Jesus was and is a faithful Jew and the bigger the Messianic movement becomes, the more visible these ideas will be.

Eventually, though, influential Christian teachers must begin to embrace the Jewish Jesus. The big names, the popular names, the ones we see on television and whose books are sold at Wal-Mart need to seriously examine the roots of their faith and study the first-century church to see that Jesus and the apostles never meant to wipe out Judaism. These influential men and women must begin to teach that early Jewish disciples of Jesus continued to practice Judaism and that Gentile disciples of Jesus considered themselves part of a multinational extension of Israel.

You may think that I am joking. I have to admit that what I'm proposing is very difficult. It is uncommon for Christian leaders to retract something central to what they have taught or to make big changes in their theology. If people believe in something so strongly that they are willing to shout it from the mountaintops to millions of listeners, readers, and followers, they are not likely to change that belief.

But "with God all things are possible" (Matthew 19:26). I am sure that when Paul wrote Romans 11, he could never have imagined that the Jewish people would "stumble" for so long because of the actions of Jesus' followers. However, I am also certain that Paul saw God's endgame. He writes of the Jewish people, "They too have now been disobedient in order that by the mercy shown to you [Gentile believers in Jesus] they also may now receive mercy. For God has consigned all to disobedience, that he may have mercy on all" (Romans 11:31–32).

By the mercy shown to us, the Jewish people will receive mercy. I believe that in the end the Jewish people will see Jesus for who he is—not because we have enticed them away from Judaism and into Christianity, but because we have rediscovered who Jesus is and embraced Jesus the Jewish rabbi as our Master and Teacher and Lord. The "deposit" of Jesus' life and teaching will have finally matured within the church, and the Jewish people will collect what was originally theirs to begin with.

Why do influential Christians have to pick up this banner? Because this change has to be so comprehensive and has to affect such a huge percentage of Christians that Jesus' identity becomes clear to everyone in the world. The people the world looks to as leaders, definers, and spokespeople for the Christian faith have to bear this burden.

But that involves a serious sea change, a turnaround from what we have taught and believed for two thousand years. It requires repentance. It requires humility and the ability to say, "I was wrong."

With God all things are possible.

# Embracing the Torah

*Moses came and told the people all the words of the LORD and all the rules. And all the people answered with one voice and said, "All the words that the LORD has spoken we will do."*

— *Exodus 24:3*

In this book and in *Yeshua Matters*, I have purposefully avoided going into great detail on the subject of the Mosaic Law. That subject is covered in the next book in this series, appropriately titled *Torah Matters*.

However, while we are discussing the relationship between the church and the Jewish people, we must at least touch on the topic of the Law, the Torah.

One of the many covenants God made with the Jewish people was the Mosaic covenant, also called the Sinai covenant. In this covenant, God gave the Jewish people 613 commandments (according to the traditional Jewish count). He also gave them promises and blessings that were contingent on their obedience to those commandments.

This covenant was not like the Abrahamic covenant. Once Abraham left Ur for Canaan, God's promises of blessing were eternally secured for the Jewish people. The Sinai covenant, in contrast, requires continual obedience, generation after generation. As part of the Sinai covenant, God offered the Torah, a certain way of life, to the Jewish people, and they accepted it. Under that covenant, the

Jewish people must continually obey the Torah in order to receive the blessings of God and remain in their land.

If they do not obey, the Torah outlines penalties, consequences, and judgments.

The blessings and curses of the Torah are summed up in Deuteronomy 11:

> If you will indeed obey my commandments that I command you today, to love the LORD your God, and to serve him with all your heart and with all your soul, he will give the rain for your land in its season, the early rain and the later rain, that you may gather in your grain and your wine and your oil. And he will give grass in your fields for your livestock, and you shall eat and be full. Take care lest your heart be deceived, and you turn aside and serve other gods and worship them; then the anger of the LORD will be kindled against you, and he will shut up the heavens, so that there will be no rain, and the land will yield no fruit, and you will perish quickly off the good land that the LORD is giving you. (Deuteronomy 11:13–17)

If you are familiar with Jewish history, you know that eventually God had to invoke the penalty clause of the Torah—he had to remove the Jewish people from the land he had promised them.

However, as we have seen throughout this book, God's unilateral promises to Abraham and to the Jewish people will eventually cause him to restore them completely. Paul put it this way: "The law, which came 430 years afterward, does not annul a covenant previously ratified by God, so as to make the promise void" (Galatians 3:17).

In other words, even though the Torah, the Mosaic Law, made God's blessings conditional on the obedience of the Jewish people, God had already promised that no matter what happened, the Jewish people would always be his people, the land of Israel would always be their land, and he would always be their God.

As we discussed earlier, God will accomplish this by causing the Jewish people to become obedient, by giving them a new heart and a new spirit (Ezekiel 36:26–28).

But what can Christians do today in light of the reality that the Jewish people remain in covenant with God and subject to the laws of the Torah?

# Encouragers

The Bible makes it clear that when the Jewish people live in obedience to the Torah, they are blessed. When they disobey, they are cursed. As the Apostle Paul stated, "I testify again to every man who accepts circumcision [that is, who converts to Judaism] that he is obligated to keep the whole law" (Galatians 5:3). According to Paul, all Jews must keep "the whole law," even now that Jesus has been revealed as the Messiah.[56]

If the church is a multinational extension of Israel, then how does the Jewish people's observance of the Mosaic Law figure into our relationship with them?

Basically, Christians must adopt into their theology the fact that Jewish people remain obligated to obey the Torah.

That is a dangerous thing to say. So let me qualify it a bit.

We should not badger secular or non-observant Jews to change their religion or their view of the Torah. This will do no good and will only harm our relationship with the Jewish community.

We should not, in fact, impose our will on the Jewish community at all. It is not our job to tell the Jewish people what to do.

I am talking about a theological shift, a shift in our understanding, such that we embrace the Torah as God's revealed will for the Jewish people.

This will affect the way we do church. If we believe that Jewish people should obey the Torah, then Jewish disciples of Jesus will be given an expectation that their lifestyles should gradually change to conform to obedience to the Torah. Jewish disciples of Jesus in Christian churches will be held accountable to the Torah's laws.

I am not talking about a hard-and-fast rule here. Grace is just as much a part of the life of a Jewish believer in Jesus as it is a part of the life of a non-Jewish believer in Jesus.

However, as God continues to regenerate our hearts and as we continue to grow in Christ, the ultimate goal of a Jewish disciple of Jesus should be to live in obedience to the Law of Moses, just as Jesus taught his disciples:

> Do not think that I have come to abolish the Law or the Prophets; I have not come to abolish them but to fulfill them. For truly, I say to you, until heaven and earth pass away, not an iota, not a dot, will pass from the Law until all is accomplished. Therefore whoever relaxes one of the least of these commandments and teaches others to do the same will be called least in the kingdom of heaven, but whoever does them and teaches them will be called great in the kingdom of heaven. (Matthew 5:17–19)

The Jesus-following Jew's relationship to the Torah is mediated by Jewish tradition, as Jesus also taught: "The scribes and the Pharisees sit on Moses' seat, so do and observe whatever they tell you, but not the works they do. For they preach, but do not practice" (Matthew 23:2–3).

If Jesus is right, and the scribes and Pharisees really sat on Moses' seat, then the traditional ways in which Jewish people throughout history have observed the Torah's commandments must somehow figure into the Torah-observant life of the Jewish believer in Jesus.

Those of us who are not Jewish must take the role of encouragers and enablers, making it easier for Jewish believers in Jesus to live a Jewish life, making allowances for the stringencies of Jewish law, and respecting the traditions of the Jewish community.

Sometimes this may even take the form of a financial commitment. Many Jewish laws are expensive to fulfill. The commandment to have a mezuzah (a hand-written scroll containing verses from the Bible) on every doorpost of a home, the commandment to wrap tefillin (leather boxes containing similar scrolls) around one's head and arm every morning, the commandment to write (or commission the writing of) a Torah scroll—these laws are expensive to obey, and the costs can run into the thousands of dollars.

Can you imagine how uplifting it would be to the Messianic Jewish community, though, if local churches all over the world began to give financial aid to Messianic Jewish synagogues, enabling

Jewish disciples of Jesus to lay tefillin, affix mezuzot, and commission Torah scrolls to be written?

Or what if Christian churches were to sponsor Messianic Jewish students to go to school and study the laws and traditions of the Jewish people?

Or what if Christians began to sponsor translation projects to put important Jewish texts in the hands of English-speaking Jews? How encouraging would that be to the Messianic Jewish community?

And what about the broader impact on the Jewish community? What would it say about Jesus and his followers? How long would we still be seen as the destroyers of Judaism?

Can you see how supporting the Jewish people in their observance of the Torah is a necessary step that we must take in order to restore the reputation of Jesus and to repair our relationship with the Jewish people?

# Kingdom

In an earlier chapter we discussed the kingdom of heaven. When non-Jews attach themselves to the Jewish Messiah, they become part of his kingdom. They become part of the domain in which God's rule is active and manifest in the world.

In a future time, in the Messianic Age, the kingdom of heaven will encompass the whole world. Everyone on earth will know that Jesus is the King over all creation. Everyone will know that they are subject to his rule. God's kingdom will fully break into the present reality.

This has always been God's endgame. The plan to restore and redeem the world through Jesus dates back to before the dawn of time. God will rescue his physical creation and plant us in a perfect world.

In that world all of God's people will obey him. Our hearts and spirits will be recreated, and we will be perfect. If we were to remain sinful, we would inflict damage on the redeemed and restored world that God is going to create. Sin cannot be allowed in the kingdom of heaven. God's will must be done perfectly in order for paradise, a place of eternal reward for the faithful, to exist.

God has hinted as to what this world will be like—as we would expect, in the Prophets, but also in the Torah, in the Mosaic Law. The kingdom of heaven allows no murder, no unfaithfulness, no hatred toward one another, no idolatry. The commandments of the Torah describe that ideal world.

When God gave the Torah to the Jewish people, he gave them the responsibility to demonstrate what the kingdom of heaven looks like to the other nations of the world. Through living out the Torah, the nation of Israel was to be a beacon of righteousness, a light in the midst of a world darkened by sin and idolatry:

> See, I have taught you statutes and rules, as the LORD my God commanded me, that you should do them in the land that you are entering to take possession of it. Keep them and do them, for that will be your wisdom and your understanding in the sight of the peoples, who, when they hear all these statutes, will say, "Surely this great nation is a wise and understanding people." For what great nation is there that has a god so near to it as the LORD our God is to us, whenever we call upon him? And what great nation is there, that has statutes and rules so righteous as all this law that I set before you today? (Deuteronomy 4:5–8)

Christians have long taught that the Jewish people and the Torah have both lost these pivotal roles in God's larger plan. However, as I hope we have learned, the Jewish people remain the people of God, and, as you will learn if you continue on and read *Torah Matters*, the Torah remains their covenantal obligation. The responsibility to show the world what the kingdom of heaven looks like still falls on the Jewish people, and the Torah remains the instrument that God has chosen for them to accomplish this task.

Moses spoke confidently of the role of the Torah in the coming redemption, even before the Jewish people were ever exiled from their land:

> The LORD your God will circumcise your heart and the heart of your offspring, so that you will love the LORD your God with all your heart and with all your soul, that you may live. ... And you shall again obey the voice of the

LORD and keep all his commandments that I command you today. (Deuteronomy 30:6, 8)

When God breaks through into history and redeems the Jewish people, they will be completely faithful to the commandments of the Torah. But until that time, the Jewish people's observance of the Torah is still a key piece of God's revelation of himself to humanity. The witness of the Jewish people to the world is a key part of their mission and of the larger kingdom mission to redeem and restore everything.

Christians have their own responsibilities in this kingdom mission. One of them is to live out our own witness in submission to God's rule—and this lifestyle is also defined by the Torah, the law of the kingdom, although Gentiles do not have exactly the same responsibilities under the Torah that Jewish people do.

But another key part of our mission as Gentile believers in Jesus is to help and encourage Jewish people to live out the commandments of the Torah. In doing so we further God's cause. We expand the kingdom of heaven. We bring the final redemption closer. We make the world around us a little more like the perfect world that is coming.

# Israel's Salvation

*Jesus said to him, "I am the way, and the truth, and the life. No one comes to the Father except through me."*

— John 14:6

This book is not a theological treatise on salvation or on heaven and hell. When I originally set out to write it, I was only going to address the corporate nation of Israel and her covenant relationship with God. But I quickly found that when one cracks the egg of Christian ecclesiology and begins to explore the eternal role and calling of the Jewish people apart from the historical teaching of the church, he risks making a mess: the yolk of soteriology— the doctrine of salvation—immediately begins to seep out.

For that reason I have repeated throughout this book that we will at some point address the critical questions that are inevitably raised whenever someone claims that the Jewish people are still the people of God, that they are still beneficiaries of God's promises and party to God's covenants:

- Are Jewish people saved, down to the last person, because of God's covenant with Abraham? Even if they don't believe in Jesus?
- If so, does that mean they are saved in a different way than Christians are saved?

- If there is hope for Jewish people who do not believe in Jesus, then is there hope for members of the nations who have never heard of Jesus?
- Where do we draw the line that differentiates between who is "in" and who is "out"—who has eternal life and who doesn't?

I have saved these questions for the last chapter, because I don't believe that theological discussion is fruitful until we have a good biblical foundation from which to work. The pool of Scripture that we draw from to address these questions needs to be wider than the Epistle to the Romans and the Gospel of John. We can develop a very good argument from a few Bible verses only to see it demolished by a few more. So our theology needs to be informed by the whole narrative arc encompassed by the Bible—the whole story—rather than just a few famous verses.

I hope that through investigating the major groups of people defined in the Bible, I have helped to lay this narrative foundation. We will see whether that foundation is helpful as we address these pressing questions.

We'll start with an easy question: is every Jewish person automatically saved?

## *Hereditary*

From verses that say "all Israel will be saved" (Romans 11:26) and "Israel is saved by the LORD with everlasting salvation" (Isaiah 45:17), along with the powerful promises in Jeremiah 30–31 and Ezekiel 36, it would be easy to assume that every Jewish person will inherit eternal life—that because of their membership in the Jewish community, they inherit a hereditary kind of personal salvation; they are automatically "in."

But we know that this isn't the case. Consider the message of John the Baptist, for example:

When he saw many of the Pharisees and Sadducees coming to his baptism, he said to them, "You brood of vipers! Who warned you to flee from the wrath to come? Bear fruit in keeping with repentance. And do not presume to say to yourselves, 'We have Abraham as our father,' for I tell you, God is able from these stones to raise up children for Abraham. Even now the axe is laid to the root of the trees. Every tree therefore that does not bear good fruit is cut down and thrown into the fire." (Matthew 3:7–10)

Here John confronts a belief that some Jewish people held in his day: that all Jews will have a place in the World to Come simply because they are Jewish, because they inherit God's covenant with Abraham. There is no room for this belief in John's theology. With a prophetic voice he condemns unrepentant Pharisees and Sadducees to a fiery punishment. Jewish people who failed to repent, who failed to bear good fruit, were not going to inherit the kingdom of heaven.

Paul, alluding to this same truth, wrote in Romans 9:6 that "not all who are descended from Israel belong to Israel." That is, not every person descended from the person Israel (the patriarch Jacob) belongs to the eschatological kingdom of Israel (the final expression of the national kingdom of Israel as it will exist during the Messianic Age—a kingdom which, in Paul's theology, was somehow breaking into reality in his lifetime).

In other words, God reserves the right to deny salvation to some individual Jews. But this does not mean that the entire Jewish nation will be condemned unless they reject Jewishness and Judaism in favor of Christianity. For Paul also wrote that "all Israel will be saved" (Romans 11:26).

Here's how German scholar Johannes Munck explained the tension between Israel's salvation and the denial of this salvation to some individual Jews:

> "All Israel" denotes "the remnant" [Jesus-believing Jews] together with "the rest" [non-Jesus-believing Jews] (cf. 11:5–7), and although it stands in contrast to "the remnant," there is no question of completeness. All the categories of *Heilsgeschichte*—the Gentiles and Israel, the "remnant," and the church—are saved or rejected in their entirety, but the salvation of the individual cannot be assumed from God's election and salvation of the

particular totality to which he belongs. The fate of the individual is determined by Christ at the Judgment.[57]

As we explore the fate of the Jewish people corporately versus the fate of individual Jewish persons, it is useful to draw an analogy from the fate of the Christian church corporately versus the fate of individual Christian persons. As Munck points out, both the church and Israel are promised salvation, but both individual Christians and Jews are in a more precarious situation; they cannot assume they will inherit eternal life because of their membership in a group. This is best illustrated by a selection from the Sermon on the Mount:

> Not everyone who says to me, "Lord, Lord," will enter the kingdom of heaven, but the one who does the will of my Father who is in heaven. On that day many will say to me, "Lord, Lord, did we not prophesy in your name, and cast out demons in your name, and do many mighty works in your name?" And then will I declare to them, "I never knew you; depart from me, you workers of lawlessness." (Matthew 7:21–23)

This is a scary passage, and any attempt to make it less scary guts it of its meaning. Jesus teaches very clearly that many people who are members of the Christian church and identifiable as believers in Jesus, and even many who are able to perform miracles in the name of Jesus, will not find their personal final destiny a happy one. Whatever specific reasons we might posit for their damnation or whatever theological framework we may try to create in order to remove this startling tension, we must wrestle with this critical fact: Jesus apparently intended his disciples to understand that their eternal destiny was not guaranteed by their membership in a group (that is, the Christian church) or their affiliation with a religion (what we today call Christianity).[58]

In the same way, individual Jewish people are not guaranteed salvation because of their membership in a group—in their case, Israel—or their participation in a religion (Judaism). However, both the church and Israel have corporately been given eschatological promises that God must fulfill in order to keep his word. The exceptions God makes in the cases of some individuals do not invalidate the promises given to the groups corporately.

Perhaps the most difficult part of this idea, for Protestants at least, is the *basis* on which those exceptions are made, the basis on which God chooses to condemn individual Jews and Christians. Matthew 7 (and other passages in the Synoptic Gospels about the final judgment and/or the fate of the dead—see Matthew 24–25 and Luke 16) heavily imply that some Christians and Jews will be damned on the basis of what they have done or failed to do: "Not everyone who says to me, 'Lord, Lord,' will enter the kingdom of heaven, but the one who *does* the will of my Father who is in heaven" (Matthew 7:21, emphasis added).

But as we wrote above, when we begin to reassess the doctrine of individual salvation with our expanded pool of texts—not just John and Romans but the rest of the Bible—we will find that some arguments just don't hold up. And one of those untenable arguments is that everyone who believes that Jesus is the Messiah will automatically get to live forever.

In fact, I would argue that instead of speculating as to whether individual Jewish people will be saved, it would be a better use of our time for each of us to speculate as to whether we as individuals will be saved. I see no passage in the Bible that gives the church license to condemn every non-Jesus-believing Jewish person to hell for failing to recognize Jesus as the Messiah. However, I do see clearly in Matthew 7 the mandate for Christians to continually reassess their *own* candidacy for salvation.

## Spokes

As soon as we suggest that Israel will be saved on the basis of her covenant with God, given to Abraham in Genesis 17, we fall prey to the accusation that we make all religions equal. Like spokes on a wheel, someone will say, this writer believes that all religions begin in different places but find their end in a saving relationship with God.

This is not the case at all. The idea that Israel will corporately be granted a place in the World to Come is simply drawn from what the Bible says clearly over and over. We may be painting ourselves into a corner here, but we do so by following the paint scheme God gave us.

Perhaps a more pertinent question is this: is the basis for Israel's salvation different from the basis for the church's salvation? In other words, does God have two different plans of salvation? Or, to move from the corporate to the individual level, do Jewish people need Jesus to be saved?

The Apostle John recorded these words of Jesus: "I am the way, and the truth, and the life. No one comes to the Father except through me" (John 14:6).

But Israel has not corporately accepted Jesus as the Messiah. So how can Israel be saved? And how can individual Jewish people inherit a happy final destiny if they do not believe in Jesus? Do they have to choose between the Gospel of John and the prophecies of Jeremiah and Ezekiel?

Some of the early church fathers reconciled this difficulty by claiming that Christians are the true spiritual Israel and that only Christians will be saved. But we can't accept this, based on our studies in previous chapters. The nation of Israel has been given promises of her own that God cannot break.

The dispensationalist answer is that Israel will corporately convert to Christianity and then, as a consequence, all Israel will be saved. The earthly people of Judaism will become part of the heavenly people of Christianity, the church, the body of faith. But this leaves no permanent or lasting role for the people of Israel *as Israel*, as Jews. In dispensationalist thought Jewish people lose their identity and their unique calling when they accept Jesus. Before they receive Christ they only exist as a catalyst for some end-time prophecies. Afterward they don't exist as a definable entity at all. All the wonderful promises of a rescued people of Israel in a renewed land of Israel under the restored king of Israel fall flat in this paradigm.

So let us state our premises, drawn from earlier chapters, along with John 14:6, and see if we can come up with a better solution:

1. Israel will be saved forever because of God's promises to Abraham.

2. The church will be saved forever because she is "in Christ."

3. No individual person can "come to the Father" except through Jesus.

We have already explored the first two premises. But the third raises some questions that we haven't yet asked or answered. Namely, is this statement, that Jesus is the only way to the Father, a statement that is true of all time, in all space, and of every person? If so, what ramifications does that have for our interpretation of this verse as regards soteriology—the doctrine of personal salvation from sin and death?

To use an example, did Abraham also have to go through Jesus to "come to the Father"? Does John 14:6 apply to him as well? We might think it doesn't—that Jesus must have changed the rules when he came to earth—because in Genesis, Abraham doesn't seem to need a mediator to be able to talk with God. God just speaks to Abraham, and Abraham speaks right back.

Hold on, though.

There may have been something else going on in the Abraham story, something we don't see right away in our English translation. Let's dive back into the first century and revisit some ideas that may have influenced John's choice of words in his gospel account.

In Jesus' time the language of the common people in Israel was Aramaic. But the Old Testament is mostly written in Hebrew. So to understand their Bible, the Old Testament, most Jewish people needed translations of the Old Testament into Aramaic. These translations are called Targums.

As they translated, pious scribes replaced some direct references to God in the Targums with the term *Memra* (Word), a presence that represented God's activity without referring to God personally.

John was familiar with the Targums; he would have heard them read in the synagogue every Sabbath, because these translations were read out loud, right along with the original Hebrew of the Old Testament. Hearing the Targums, he would have learned about the *Memra*, and he probably would have understood it as an active manifestation of God's activity throughout the Old Testament.

By the time John wrote his gospel, it was clear to him that Jesus was more than just a human, more than just a rabbi. As he probed the Old Testament for words and ideas to help him understand Jesus' nature and to help him explain to his readers what Jesus was, one of the ideas he settled on was the *Memra*, the Word. So the Targumic *Memra*, in John's theology, became the preexistent Jesus.

Because he saw the *Memra* as Jesus in his preexistent form, John expanded the idea of the *Memra* in his gospel in order to make it clear to his readers that Jesus had been present and active in the world throughout the entire Old Testament period. Instead of being a mere representation of God's activity, John's *Memra* has an identity of its own.

After expanding the role of the *Memra* in the first few verses of his gospel, John goes on to connect that very same *Memra* to Jesus. We must conclude that in John's theology, *Jesus mediates all God's activity in the physical world.* In other words, every time God does anything in the world, he accomplishes it through Jesus, through the Word. All of God's relationships with human beings are also mediated through the Word. Since the presence of the *Memra* extends back through Old Testament times and beyond, even God's relationship with Abraham was mediated through the Word. Through Jesus.

John reinforces this concept in verse 9 of that first chapter of his gospel: "The true light, which gives light to everyone, was coming into the world." Somehow, Jesus, the light of the world, shines on *everyone*—even on people who have never heard of him. This verse again references Jesus' role as the *Memra*, which mediates all of God's activity in the physical world.

Now let's revisit John 14:6—anyone who wants to come to the Father must go through Jesus. We normally understand this to mean that someone has to know Jesus' name, has to know Jesus personally, has to hear about and believe in the human being called Rabbi Yeshua of Nazareth in order to have a relationship with God. But if we take John at his word when he teaches that Jesus is the only way to the Father, we must also take him at his word when he teaches that Jesus is the omnipresent, preexistent Word through whom the Father always reveals himself *and has always revealed himself,* even as far back as the Genesis creation story—"all things were made through him" (John 1:3).

We butcher John's theology if we accept John 14:6, which teaches that no one comes to the Father except through Jesus, but ignore John chapter 1, which teaches that everything God has accomplished in the world has been accomplished through Jesus, and that Jesus, the true light, shines on everyone in the world.[59] If we believe John when he tells us that Jesus is our only connection with God, we also have to believe John's teaching that Jesus is God's agent *whenever God does anything* on planet Earth. John rooted both of these ideas in Jesus' identity as the eternal, preexistent *Memra*. We can't have one without the other.

If we are tracking with John correctly here, then the declaration "I am the way, and the truth, and the life; no one comes to the Father except through me" actually means something totally different than "Believe in Jesus or go to hell." Jesus is *not making a statement about how to get to heaven, or about who gets to live forever*. Instead, Jesus is making a statement about *who and what he is* in his capacity as the *Memra*, the Word through whom God's activity is mediated.

To those of us who are reading the Gospel of John expecting big revelations about Jesus and about salvation, this interpretation of John 14:6 might be kind of a letdown. But keep in mind that while we have read John chapter 1 and already know that Jesus is the Word, the disciples in John chapter 14 hadn't really grasped this idea yet. So while we may not see how significant this statement would have been at that time, or why Jesus would have needed to make this point to his disciples, we have to remember that Jesus was still in the process of revealing that he was something greater than just a rabbi or a normal human being. His disciples didn't know yet that he was God's eternal agent, God's Word, God's *Memra*.

Jesus went on to tell his disciples, "I am in the Father and the Father is in me" (John 14:10). This verse can be seen from the same perspective. As in verse 6, Jesus' point was not that the only way to know God is through knowing the human being, the incarnate Word, Jesus of Nazareth. Instead, his point was that wherever God is active, that activity is mediated through the Word—and that Word was incarnated as Jesus, or, to use Paul's terminology, the Word was the "fullness of deity" that dwelt in Jesus bodily (Colossians 2:9).

As in the preceding verses, Jesus' purpose in this passage was *to reveal his fuller identity to his disciples*, not necessarily *to condemn to eternal hellfire* all people who might never hear about or understand the human being we know as Jesus.

If I'm right, then Christian theology is still correct in its claim that everyone who is saved will be saved through Jesus—through the Word. I certainly still believe that no one can be saved without having their sins forgiven, and that no one's sins are forgiven apart from Jesus' priestly work of mediation. But this does not necessarily mean that every person who is saved will have died knowing about the historical person of Jesus of Nazareth.

Again, I am not suggesting that salvation is available through any other way than Jesus—he is the way, the truth, and the life. But I am suggesting that salvation through Jesus may be available to someone who does not have the cognitive ability to understand Jesus' fuller identity, or to someone who doesn't have access to information that would allow them to develop an understanding of Jesus of Nazareth as the manifestation of God's Word.

If we interpret John in this way, in light of first-century Jewish terminology, we make room for God to work in Israel through Jesus in his capacity as the eternal Word, even though the Jewish people may not understand or accept the historical figure of Jesus of Nazareth as the Messiah. This does not mean that Jews get saved in a different way, or under a different covenant; ultimately, they are saved through Jesus, by the grace of God, just as Jesus' non-Jewish disciples are. As Peter said, "But we believe that we [the Jewish people] will be saved through the grace of the Lord Jesus, just as they [Jesus-believing Gentiles] will" (Acts 15:11). But through his mysterious and hidden role as the omnipresent Word, Jesus' grace may be available to a Jewish person who has never heard about the historical person of Jesus, or who does not understand why Jesus must be the Messiah.[60]

I know this is a difficult pill to swallow. But if we're honest, we already believe this about several other kinds of people. Many of those who died before Jesus rose from the dead, those who die before they old enough to understand anything about Jesus, the severely mentally handicapped, and aborted or miscarried children—I know of no Christian who would categorically condemn all these groups of people to eternal punishment. Even the most theologically conservative Christians must admit that all of us already expect Jesus to grant eternal life to *some* people who do not know him personally. I am just extending this possibility to the Jewish people on the basis of their covenant relationship with God—the same covenant that ultimately makes eternal life available to the Gentiles, the "new covenant" of Jeremiah 31:31–34, promised to Israel millennia ago.

Many Christians now acknowledge that the land of Israel has been granted as a permanent possession to the Jewish people.[61] Their belief is based on God's unconditional promises to the Jewish people. All we are doing here is taking the same logic—an acknowledgement of the continuing validity of God's promises regarding the *land* of Israel—and applying it to the promises of corporate salvation that God made to the *people* of Israel.

Now maybe I'm wrong. That could very well be. And I also realize that opening the door for Jesus to work among the Jewish people "incognito" also opens up a Pandora's box of problems, a swarm of unanswerable questions regarding which other people might attain eternal life and how. I cannot address these questions here. I only broached the subject of individual salvation in this book because our theology needs some way to reconcile how God can save the corporate people of Israel, as he has absolutely and irrevocably promised to do, and at the same time remain true to what the New Testament teaches about Jesus, about individual final destinies, and about the permanent continuation of Jewish identity.

But before we go on, let's consider a section of Romans. In chapters 9 through 11, Paul makes an impassioned defense of God's actions in delaying the salvation of the Jewish people. The thrust of his argument over these three chapters is that the corporate people of Israel will be saved, but that this salvation has been delayed because the Messiah King was not put on his rightful throne at the time of his coming. As a result, many individual Jewish people lost the opportunity to see the final redemption of the nation of Israel. However, the eternal destiny of the nation as a whole is secure; God will choose to extend mercy to the Jewish people at some future time.

Part of Paul's theodicy, his defense of God, is his argument that God is not obligated to grant every Jewish person eternal life. He introduces this concept in Romans 2 and revisits it in Romans 9. But let's turn this passage on its head for a moment:

> What shall we say then? Is there injustice on God's part? By no means! For he says to Moses, "I will have mercy on whom I have mercy, and I will have compassion on whom

I have compassion." So then it depends not on human will or exertion, but on God, who has mercy. For the Scripture says to Pharaoh, "For this very purpose I have raised you up, that I might show my power in you, and that my name might be proclaimed in all the earth." So then he has mercy on whomever he wills, and he hardens whomever he wills. (Romans 9:14–18)

Paul is likening the non-Jesus-believing Jews of his time period to Pharaoh. They have been hardened for a specific purpose in salvation history.

But consider the last verse in that passage. God "has mercy on whomever he wills, and he hardens whomever he wills." As evangelical Christians, we have consistently taught that God's mercy on a person, as Paul speaks of it in this passage, is revealed through their acceptance of Jesus as the Messiah; we believe this because we believe that God will have mercy only on believers in Jesus. But that is not Paul's point—not yet, not in this part of the chapter. Pharaoh would be a terrible example of that principle; he lived before Jesus was born.

Paul is making a more general point in this section of Romans 9. He is saying that *God can do whatever he wants*, and we just have to *deal with it*. We can't make any sort of claim on God that he should save or not save any one person in particular. The final judgment is between Jesus and the person being judged and, as we have already seen in passages like Matthew 25:31–46, this judgment hinges on factors other than a person's creed, race, or religious orientation. "Come, you who are blessed by my Father, inherit the kingdom prepared for you from the foundation of the world. *For I was hungry and you gave me food…*" (Matthew 25:34–35, emphasis added).

So God can refuse to grant eternal life to some individual Jewish people, and the Jewish people as a whole have no right to complain; "he hardens whomever he wills." This is what Paul is getting at in Romans 9. But we can use the very same principle to argue that God can also choose to save the Jewish people corporately, and even to grant eternal life to individual Jewish people, and Christians have no right to complain: "He has mercy on whomever he wills."

I think this concept is difficult for many evangelical Protestants because we have reduced Jesus' role to that of atonement. He is the sacrifice that atones for our sins, paving the way for God to accept us into his family.

What I'm about to say may not be true of formal evangelical systematic theology, but it seems to me that in our practical application of that theology, Jesus has become a passive agent in the salvation process. He is somehow not in control; he is obligated to save people who believe his claims about himself, and to condemn people who never hear about him. Instead of his followers belonging to him, as sheep in a sheepfold, Jesus belongs to us, as if he were some sort of password to our salvation.

Let us not forget that Jesus is the judge, the final decider, who has "all authority in heaven and on earth" (Matthew 28:18). If we are to believe Jesus' account of the final judgment in Matthew 25, Jesus himself is the final arbiter of salvation. He is not a powerless pawn caught in a heartless salvation machine by which people are trapped in heaven or hell based on a loophole, a prayer, a religious belief, or a lack thereof. Jesus is the active agent, the righteous judge, the decider. He gets to pick. And he can pick whomever he wants. We don't get to argue with him over who should get picked and who shouldn't. We are his property; he is not ours.

When we read Genesis 17 and the promises of the prophets in Jeremiah 30–31, Ezekiel 36, and elsewhere, we must consider the possibility that Jesus, the preexistent Word, revealed in advance through these Scriptures that he had already picked the Jewish people. After all, he is their King, and they are his people. Is it so hard to believe that he will come through for them? He has promised as much.

# Unbeliever

On my way to work, I like to turn on the alternative radio station. I think pastors should get to know the culture they are reaching out to, but I also make no apology for enjoying some of the tunes.

One song that has been playing a lot lately is by a band called Vampire Weekend. The song is "Unbelievers." It goes like this:

> We know the fire awaits unbelievers,
> All of the sinners, the same. ...
> I'm not excited, but should I be?

Is this the fate that half of the world has planned for me?

Many Christians may wonder why the songwriter had this cynical response to the "good news" of Jesus. But I don't wonder. I imagine that when he heard the gospel, it sounded something like this: "Good news, everyone! You're all going to burn in hell forever, but if you act now, and join our religion, you won't have to go there after all!"

You might think that I am trivializing the gospel message. Truly I'm not. My life has been utterly transformed by the good news of Jesus Christ. But we have to be aware of how our culture is responding to the message we are sending them. Their response is not always pretty, but we don't accomplish anything by getting offended—the kingdom of heaven is not advanced by hurt feelings over a rejection of our message. Truthfully, sometimes we get a negative response because we don't get the message quite right to begin with.

I say this to preface the last section in this chapter. I want to touch on John 3:18: "Whoever believes in him is not condemned, but whoever does not believe is condemned already, because he has not believed in the name of the only Son of God."

This verse makes it sound as if everyone who does not believe in the name of the Son of God—that is, the name "Jesus"—is condemned. Hell-bound. Fuel for the fire.

In contrast, everyone who does believe in the name of Jesus is guaranteed eternal life.

But wait, we know, because we just read Matthew 7:21–23 a few pages ago, that not everyone who believes that Jesus is the Messiah is guaranteed salvation. Some of them will get the "I never knew you" speech. They will be shocked and confused by Jesus' reaction when they come before him relying on their religious affiliation for salvation.

And then we are stuck with the response of the people we witness to—the people who are disconcerted with the idea that God would throw someone in hell (forever) or admit him to heaven (forever) based on their reaction to a *piece of information that not everyone has access to*: "Jesus is the Messiah." And this cynical response is hard for us to deal with, because something doesn't really sit well with this whole salvation economy in our spirits either.

Somewhere, deep inside, I think that most of us know that the name of Jesus must be more than a magic word that brings eternal life.

So is John talking about something different here? Is it possible that we have simply misunderstood him?

The phrase "the name of the only Son of God" seems very clear to most evangelical Christians. But maybe this is because we have been taught from spiritual infancy, as I was, that the actual name of "Jesus" is what saves people from their sins.

Maybe this phrase meant something else to John.

To review a bit from *Yeshua Matters*, the words and phrases we find in the Gospels often carry meanings that we would never discover on our own. These terms are drawn from the culture and world of first-century Judaism, and if we are not familiar with that world, we will miss the intended meaning. Even if the words are translated correctly, idioms—like a "New York minute" or a "baker's dozen"—are not defined by the actual words they contain. Over time, they develop their own unique definitions. So we can't understand these kinds of phrases by just reading the words. We have to learn what they mean in the same way we learn what new words mean—by reading a dictionary or by hearing them used in conversation.

As we wrote above, John's Christology is, at least in part, informed by the Targums, Aramaic translations of the Old Testament. He makes this clear in the first few verses of his gospel in which he calls Jesus the Word—the *Memra*, a term drawn from the Targums.

Johannine scholar John Ronning, author of a landmark study on John's *Memra* theology, noted that "the name of the *Memra* of God" is a phrase found over and over in the Targums. When this phrase is used, it actually refers to the Tetragrammaton, the four-letter personal name of God that traditional Jews do not pronounce except in very narrow circumstances.[62]

So while it seems obvious to today's Christian reader of the Gospel of John that the "name of the only Son of God" is the personal name of the rabbi from Nazareth ("Jesus"), and that everyone must know that name and learn specifically about that rabbi in order to inherit eternal life, John may well have intended to echo the language of the Targums, and to teach that people must believe in the name of the *Memra* (the Word) of the LORD in order to be saved.

What does it mean to believe in the name of the Word of the LORD? Does it mean that we need to know God's personal name?

No. This phrase is yet another idiom. It means something that we wouldn't normally understand it to mean based on the literal meanings of the individual words. But in the culture and time in which John wrote, the idiom would have been understood and interpreted properly. The meaning of the idiom "to believe in the name of the Word of the LORD" is *to respond in faith and obedience to what God has revealed.*[63]

So let's look at that verse again: "Whoever does not believe is condemned already, because he has not believed in the name of the only Son of God." To believe in the name of God's Word is to respond in faith and obedience to what God has revealed. So this verse teaches that whoever does not respond to God's revelation will be condemned. But this response will look different for different people depending on how much of himself God reveals to them.

When Jesus Christ is revealed to us, the faithful and obedient response is to accept Jesus as the Messiah King, to put our faith and trust in him, and to live in obedience to his teachings. But if someone never hears about Jesus, to "believe in the name of the Word of the LORD," or even to "believe in the name of the only Son of God," would be to respond in faith and obedience to whatever God *does* reveal to them.[64]

In the case of Cornelius the Gentile, before he met Peter God had revealed to him that he (the God of Israel) was the Creator God and the only God worthy of worship. Cornelius responded to this revelation in obedience and faith, and according to Peter's own words in Acts 10:34–35, Cornelius was accepted by God as a result.

So what about our faithful Jew, who prayed for forgiveness of sins in 26 CE and again in 34 CE, but in the meantime never heard of Jesus or had the opportunity to respond to him in a meaningful way? We cannot say that God will hold him accountable for something God did not reveal to him. He will be held accountable for his response to what God *did* reveal to him: the Old Testament—the Law and the Prophets.

We may even speculate that our uncontacted tribesman, according to Romans 1, is held responsible for his response to the work of creation itself—the implication that there exists a Creator

God who cannot be a created idol. This is all God revealed to him, so this is what God will hold him accountable for.

In any case, if John drew his terminology in this passage from the Targums (from which he also drew his "Word" theology), then to "believe in the name of the only Son of God" is to respond in obedience and faith to whatever God reveals to a person.

For an evangelical Christian, this interpretation is not intuitive. It doesn't make a lot of sense. It doesn't mesh well with evangelical theology. But evangelical theology was built without an understanding of the Targums, without an understanding of the language and terminology John was using—really, without an understanding of the Jewish context of the New Testament. And as I've been arguing for nearly two books now, the person of Jesus, understood in his original context, trumps our theology. Our doctrine is dependent on Jesus; the better we understand him, the more accurate our theology will be. Instead of trying to cram Jesus or his teachings into our theological framework, we should be continually revising our theology in response to our growing understanding of Jesus.

If we have prioritized doctrine over the living Jesus Christ, then revising our theology will be a painful and perhaps even impossible task. We will feel free to let Jesus shape our theology only if we put Jesus at the center of our faith, and let everything else revolve around him.

## Demarcation

I understand that this proposed theological shift will be impossible for many evangelical Christians to accept. The belief that Jesus' followers go to heaven and everyone else goes to hell is foundational to evangelical Christianity. Our message hinges on the existence of a thick black line between "saved" and "unsaved"; we are largely defined by an evangelistic impulse to get people over the line onto "our" side.

But this "gospel" is not so clear when we go back to the Scriptures. Instead, we see Jesus teaching his followers not to assume that their affiliation with him will grant them eternal life (Matthew 7). We have God's unilateral promises to the Jewish people that they will have a place in the World to Come (Jeremiah 30–31, Ezekiel 36).

We have Paul's reminder that Jesus can save whomever he wants to (Romans 9). We have an account of the final judgment that does not appear to hinge on beliefs but rather on actions (Matthew 25). Finally, we now have reason to suspect that the "belief" we see so often in John's gospel is not the dividing line we have made it out to be. The few verses to which we appeal to build our gospel message of "believe in Jesus and go to heaven; otherwise, go to hell" may not mean what they initially appear to mean to our twenty-first-century evangelical Christian eyes.

Ultimately this means that we cannot authoritatively distinguish between the recipients of eternal life and those who will be resurrected only to be judged and condemned. To answer the question, "where do we draw the line between saved and unsaved?" we respond that we don't get to draw that line at all. Like wheat and tares, those who are part of the eternal kingdom and those who are not grow up together in the same field (Matthew 13:24–30)—in the same denominations, in the same churches, in the same Bible-study groups—and, at least in Jesus' time, in the same synagogues.

Just as the master of the field instructed his servants to let the wheat and tares grow up together, so we as Christ's servants do not have the authority to make judgments about which people are wheat and which ones are tares and who is going where when they die. Jesus alone has been given that authority. To condemn or vindicate individuals based on religious affiliation or beliefs—or indeed for any reason at all—is to usurp Jesus' authority.

Don't get me wrong; we must boldly preach the message of repentance from sin and faith toward God through Jesus Christ, and we must boldly proclaim that God's judgment will fall upon all who hear but do not respond to his message. But when we condemn individual people, we cross the line. And to condemn the Jewish people corporately puts us on especially dangerous ground, considering how close they are to God's heart.

Imagine a father's dejection if his adopted son were to demand that he disinherit his natural-born son. He loves both his children, and ultimately, only he has the right to decide how to divide his inheritance. How impertinent it would be for one son to attempt to set his father against the other! If we respect our earthly fathers in such matters, how much more must we respect our heavenly Father's decision to remain faithful to the Jewish people?

As Paul wrote:

> Do not become proud, but fear. For if God did not spare
> the natural branches, neither will he spare you. Note then
> the kindness and the severity of God: severity toward
> those who have fallen, but God's kindness to you, pro-
> vided you continue in his kindness. Otherwise you too
> will be cut off. (Romans 11:20–22)

Do our attitudes toward the Jewish people, the "natural
branches," testify that we "continue in his kindness"? Or have we
become proud?

I offer this chapter to help the reader envision the possibility
that God is still at work among the Jewish people and to help the
reader understand how that idea might be reconciled with the
saving work that Jesus Christ alone can accomplish in the life of
an individual. I think it is possible, even though the Jewish people
corporately do not know Jesus, that he may still be the mediator
and connection between God and the Jewish people, and that he
may always have been this connection, even before his incarna-
tion, as the omnipresent *Memra*. To deny this possibility is to deny
the very nature of Jesus as the preexistent Word. It is to deny his
oneness with the same Father who called Abraham, parted the Red
Sea, and spoke to Israel through the prophets.

I could be wrong. I don't have all the answers. And you certainly
don't have to agree with me. But I do know that if our theology has
no place for the Jewish people to be once and for all the people of
God, then we've missed something. We might be able to arrange
several Bible verses in a sensible matrix to "prove" that God has
abandoned the Jews to their fate, but in doing so, I argue that we
subvert the clear message of the Law and the Prophets. A few care-
fully selected verses from the New Testament cannot be allowed to
rewrite the entire story of Israel; our interpretation of the Gospels
and Epistles must not annul God's clear promises throughout the
Old Testament.

As the prophet Jeremiah wrote:

> Thus says the LORD: "If the heavens above can be mea-
> sured, and the foundations of the earth below can be

explored, then I will cast off all the offspring of Israel for all that they have done, declares the LORD." (Jeremiah 31:37)

The Apostle Paul agrees: as regards the Jewish people, corporately, "They are beloved for the sake of their forefathers. For the gifts and the calling of God are irrevocable" (Romans 11:28–29).

# A Final Word

*Then the true self of this strange people …*
*will be revealed to all. They will recognize*
*in it all that which, since the Choice and in*
*all vicissitudes, it has never ceased to be: the*
*first-born Child, the Son—Israel the Beloved.*

— *Lev Gillet*

I wrote *Yeshua Matters* to help people meet Jesus the way I met Jesus—to encounter him as the Jewish rabbi from Nazareth.

Seeing Jesus as a Jewish rabbi raises a lot of questions. I have tried to answer some of them in this book; namely, those that relate to the Jewish people, their relationship with God, and their relationship with the church—or at least the relationship they would ideally have with the church.

Christianity began as a sect of Judaism. It was never designed to be anything different, but something different is what it became. The great divorce between Judaism and Christianity may have been avoidable, but it doesn't matter now. Jews and Christians have spiraled away from each other for the better part of two thousand years.

I think that this was part of God's plan. I think we could have handled it better, but I also think that God planned a sort of "time-out," a separation period.

During the last two thousand years, most people have forgotten why Jesus was crucified in the first place: as a result of the political ambitions of the Herodians, the Sadducees, and a select group of corrupt, wealthy, hypocritical Pharisees. Jesus was handed over to be crucified by members of a political power bloc in order to maintain the status quo that was keeping them wealthy and fed.

That power bloc was crushed in 70 CE along with the entire political structure from which it drew its sustenance. Nothing remains of it whatsoever.

In the meantime, however, Christians have adopted a "We're right, you're wrong" attitude toward the Jewish people. We have blamed them for rejecting Jesus. We have taught that Jesus came to do away with Judaism and that the Jewish people no longer have a covenant relationship with God.

Over the past few centuries of academic research into the New Testament and its context, an increasing number of scholars and researchers have found that these anti-Jewish ideas cannot be clearly traced back to Jesus or to the apostles. Replacement theology and its many offshoots all crept into the church later on, as we created a theological framework in which we became the only recipients of God's grace, and in which the Jewish people lost everything that God had promised them over many centuries through the prophets.

With what we know now, the time has come for us to restore the Jewish people to their rightful place in our theology, and particularly in our ecclesiology.

If we can make this restoration happen, it will be an incredible (and necessary) step toward the reconciliation of non-Jesus-believing Jews and Christians, the corporate reconciliation of the Jewish people with their Messiah King, and the redemption of the whole world. For as the Apostle Paul wrote, "If their rejection means the reconciliation of the world, what will their acceptance mean but life from the dead?" (Romans 11:15).

I dream of seeing this life from the dead come to pass. I want to see the world restored and every tear dried. I would expect, if you are a disciple of Christ, that you share this dream as well.

If we want to see this dream come true, we have to remember who Jesus is, and then we have to proclaim him from the rooftops.

But we also have to remember who we are—members of something bigger than we are, something older than we are, and something we don't get to control or direct—the "commonwealth of

Israel," which includes the Jewish people along with all those who dedicate their lives to Jesus.

The brother of Jesus wrote, "Humble yourselves before the Lord, and he will exalt you" (James 4:10). The converse is also true: "God opposes the proud" (James 4:6). I strongly believe that if we submit to the reality of our position, as those who have come alongside Israel and not as those who have superseded or replaced Israel, God will exalt and bless us. However, if we refuse to give pride of place to the Jewish people, God will oppose us.

As Paul wrote, "Do not be arrogant toward the branches [Jewish people who do not believe in Jesus]. If you are, remember it is not you who support the root, but the root that supports you" (Romans 11:18).

As Gentile followers of the Jewish Messiah, we are latecomers to God's kingdom. In the end we will receive the same eternal reward God promised to Israel; however, on this side of eternity, we are relative newcomers to God's salvation economy. While the Jewish people are in the midst of a momentary stumble, ultimately they are beloved on account of the patriarchs. We have only just come out from the idolatrous nations to embrace the God of Abraham; the Jewish people have served that God for four thousand years.

We are the branches that have only just joined the tree; the root of that tree is Jewish, and always will be.

Our mission and calling are no less important. We are still the church, the body of Christ. In fact, a better understanding of who and what we are will make us even more effective for our mission. For as we bring our theology and practice back in line with what the apostles originally intended, as we restore the portrait of the Jewish Jesus and accept the centrality of Israel in God's plan, our spiritual foundation becomes thicker and stronger, and our plat-form to reach the world becomes broader. Our faith finds deeper roots and bears better fruit. The doors to the kingdom open wider, and we draw the final redemption closer.

Because God's salvation plan *is* cosmic, it *is* universal. It is the redemption of the entire world, and that includes both Jews and Gentiles.

We must only realize, as Paul wrote in Romans 1:16, that this salvation came, and still comes, "to the Jew first."

# Endnotes

1   Here I rely on the Johannine account of Andrew's call, recorded in John 1:35–42.

2   Cf. Gary W. Burnett, *Paul and the Salvation of the Individual* (Leiden, The Netherlands: Brill, 2001), 73–80 Individual Israelites are sometimes in view, but these instances are best seen within the larger context of God's covenant with the entire nation.

3   As N.T. Wright put it, in an even narrower sense, "Protestants still regard the New Testament as in some sense or other the 'real' authority for Christians." *The New Testament and the People of God* (Minneapolis, MN: Fortress, 1992), 23.

4   It is common especially in American Protestantism to fail to see the need for adjudication—as if a body of written law (in our case, the Bible) can in fact address every conceivable situation through sheer deductive reasoning. This is an interesting problem that has an equally interesting corollary in American political culture, in which judges who establish significant precedents are often vilified as if they have coopted the role of the legislature. Yet the need for adjudication is well understood among philosophers of law. Cf. Duncan Kennedy, *A Critique of Adjudication [fin de siècle]* (Cambridge, MA: Harvard University Press, 1997), 28: "It seems implausible to describe the actual activity of judges as nothing more than applying law, at least as the notion of law application is generally understood… Judges constantly have to do something better described as making than as applying law. At a minimum, judges often have the job of resolving gaps, conflicts, or ambiguities in the system of legal norms. In some cases, no amount of reformulation based on the underlying definitions of the words composing the arguably applicable rules produces a deductively valid resolution. When it is agreed that there is a gap, conflict, or ambiguity in this sense, then it is also agreed that the judge who resolves it 'makes' a new rule and then applies it to the facts, rather than merely applying a preexisting rule… But it does not

follow, and is controverted, that judicial law making must be or is in fact 'judicial legislation.'"

5    The problem of "pervasive interpretive pluralism" is described lucidly by Christian Smith, *The Bible Made Impossible: Why Biblicism Is Not a Truly Evangelical Reading of Scripture* (Grand Rapids, MI: Brazos, 2011), 3–65.

6    Numbers 11:25 notes that the elders of the people, the adjudicating body, received the Spirit of God. So it is not as if God was absent from the adjudication process.

7    See m.*Pirkei Avot* 1:1.

8    So argues Mark Kinzer, *Postmissionary Messianic Judaism: Redefining Christian Engagement with the Jewish People* (Grand Rapids, MI: Brazos, 2005), 251. Contrast Anthony J. Saldarini, *Matthew's Christian-Jewish Community* (Chicago, IL: University of Chicago Press, 1994), 46–52, who argues that Jesus' seven woes against the Pharisees were included in Matthew's gospel in order to "delegitimate" (a term Saldarini prefers to "delegitimize") the post-70 CE Jewish religious leadership (i.e., those who were in the process of shaping post-Second-Temple Pharisaic/Rabbinic Judaism), a more commonly held view than that expressed here. Yet Saldarini acknowledges that this delegitimation is for the purpose of defining Matthew's Jesus-believing Jewish community as "right" against the larger Jewish community, which was "wrong" *particularly because it had not corporately accepted Jesus as the Messiah.* For this reason, even as Jesus is portrayed as the true authority throughout Matthew and is specifically contrasted with the scribes and Pharisees as titular authorities in Matthew 23, Matthew still acknowledges the social and religious structure of traditional Judaism as exemplifying the normative expression of Jewish life. To express this acknowledgement he draws on a traditional saying of Jesus (recorded in Matthew 23:2–3) that Saldarini, following a broad scholarly consensus, places within a stream of tradition preserved by Jewish believers in Jesus. Now Saldarini has Matthew disputing the Pharisees' right to adjudicate, to define Jewish life, over against the right of Matthew's community, but Matthew writes from the perspective of a community that has lost the battle—i.e., a sect that has itself been delegitimated by broader Judaism. The role of Matthew 23:2–3 in this argument is disputed, and Saldarini is ambiguous as to its purpose, offering several possibilities that fit into his thesis. Isaac Oliver, in *Torah Praxis after 70 CE: Reading Matthew and Luke/Acts as Jewish Texts* (Tübingen, Germany: Mohr Siebeck, 2013), 277 n. 117, references a widely held view that Matthew employs this saying of Jesus only because of the Pharisees' "knowledge and control of the *contents* of Scripture." Yet he disputes this interpretation on the basis of Matthew's own broad knowledge of

Scripture, preferring the view articulated here—that Jesus recognizes the authority of the Pharisees even as he attacks their conduct. Cf. the treatment of Matthew 23:2 in the Pseudo-Clementine literature: Annette Yoshiko Reed, "'Jewish Christianity' after the 'Parting of the Ways': Approaches to Historiography and Self-Definition in the Pseudo-Clementines," in *The Ways That Never Parted: Jews and Christians in Late Antiquity and the Early Middle Ages* (ed. Adam H. Becker and Annette Yoshiko Reed; Minneapolis, MN: Fortress, 2007), 222.

9 Of course, one runs into the danger of oversimplifying the state of Judaism in the first century here; in addition, the problem of the historicity of the traditional Yavneh narrative is well known. The pseudepigrapha and apocrypha as well as the DSS testify to the variegation of Jewish thought and practice in the first few centuries BCE and CE. Shaye Cohen discusses the emergence of rabbinic Judaism from this milieu in *From the Maccabees to the Mishnah* (2nd. ed.; Louisville, KY: Westminster John Knox Press, 2006); in retrospect, it is difficult if not impossible to argue that rabbinic Judaism, whenever and however it may have taken shape, did not become the normative expression of Jewish life, or that the rabbis did not conceive of themselves as carrying forward a role of adjudication similar to that which the ancient Sanhedrin had played. Whether the early rabbis were "correct" in the assumption of that role is not a question I am seeking to answer here—again, how Jewishness is defined and lived out is a subject of intra-Jewish discussion, and this recounting of the development of what may now be called "traditional" Judaism makes no attempt at a value judgment on the self-description of rabbis either ancient or modern, preferring to simply repeat the Jewish story as it is told within traditional Judaism, with the understanding that a more nuanced historical view does not substantially affect the idea that the Jewish people are the only people who can adjudicate the Jewish law, and that they have historically done so through certain defined structures. However, even as we make no value judgment on the rabbis themselves or their teachings, consider Kinzer's argument in *Postmissionary Messianic Judaism* that the reality of the continuing spiritual vitality of the Jewish people over the past two thousand years must be considered in the development of any theology of the Jewish people and their role and calling (43–44); to this Kinzer adds that the Judaism which came to define and characterize Jewish life was rabbinic Judaism (258–62). It is therefore unavoidable that in developing a Christian theology of Israel, a process toward which this book is designed to contribute, we must unavoidably rely on rabbinic Judaism to inform that theology and to inform our definition of Jewishness. Again, it is not a matter of whether the rabbis were or are right or wrong, but of the historical reality that there is no Judaism,

nor is there any definition of Jewish identity, that is not drawn in some way from rabbinic Judaism as it took shape during the time period under discussion.

10  A proper understanding of adjudication and its role in a judicial system (as defined above from Kennedy, *A Critique of Adjudication*) is absolutely necessary in order to avoid the pitfall of criticizing the Jewish body of religious tradition as if it were composed solely or primarily of additions to or even subversions of the Torah. This unwarranted criticism is rooted in a pre-critical reading of the New Testament which denies the Jewish religious identity of Jesus and the apostles, and is promulgated today by Christians who seem to me to believe that Christianity is only meaningful or "right" when contrasted against a Jewish "wrong." This perspective is increasingly in disrepute since the publication of E. P. Sanders' *Paul and Palestinian Judaism: A Comparison of Patterns of Religion* (Philadelphia, PA: Fortress, 1977), is controverted by numerous studies which have established the historical person of Jesus as a Jewish rabbi who started a movement that was consciously and deliberately defined within the parameters of Judaism, is ultimately deprecatory not only toward Judaism but toward the Jewish people, and has no place in a Messianic Jewish worldview.

11  See for example Exodus 12:43–49, which details the difference in obligation between a foreigner residing in Israel and a native born Israelite during the feast of Passover.

12  Mark D. Nanos, *The Irony of Galatians: Paul's Letter in First-Century Context* (Minneapolis, MN: Fortress, 2002), 89–91.

13  Justin Marytr, *Dialogue with Trypho* 11.

14  For specific references to these and other church fathers who embraced replacement theology, including the Justin Martyr reference above, see R. Kendall Soulen, *The God of Israel and Christian Theology* (Minneapolis, MN: Fortress, 1996), 25–56.

15  Walter Brueggemann, *A Commentary on Jeremiah: Exile & Homecoming* (Grand Rapids, MI: Eerdmans Publishing, 1998), 291–92.

16  For a more in-depth discussion, see E. P. Sanders, *Jesus and Judaism* (Philadelphia, PA: Fortress, 1985), 212–18.

17  t.*Sanhedrin* 13:2.

18  This term is explored heavily in Toby Janicki, *God-Fearers: Gentiles & the God of Israel* (Marshfield, MO: FFOZ, 2012).

19  For more background information on the centurions' role in the imperial cult, see Justin R. Howell, "The Imperial Authority and Benefaction of Centurions and Acts 10.34–43: A Response to C. Kavin Rowe," *JSNT* 31:1 (2008): 33–36.

20   Magnus Zetterholm, *The Formation of Christianity in Antioch: A Social-Scientific Approach to the Separation between Judaism and Christianity* (New York, NY: Routledge, 2003), 26–27, 128.

21   See Paula Fredriksen, *Augustine and the Jews: A Christian Defense of Jews and Judaism* (New York, NY: Doubleday, 2008), 34.

22   Cf. Alex T. Cheung, *Idol Food in Corinth: Jewish Background and Pauline Legacy* (Sheffield, England: Sheffield Academic Press, 1999), 147–152.

23   Cf. Oliver, *Torah Praxis after 70 CE*, 320–364.

24   The position outlined here is similar to the official position of the Roman Catholic Church; through phrases like "helps necessary for salvation" and "moved by grace," the dogmatic constitution quoted below indicates that God's activity among those who do not believe in Jesus has nothing to do with works-based salvation: "Those also can attain to salvation who through no fault of their own do not know the Gospel of Christ or His Church, yet sincerely seek God and moved by grace strive by their deeds to do His will as it is known to them through the dictates of conscience. Nor does Divine Providence deny the helps necessary for salvation to those who, without blame on their part, have not yet arrived at an explicit knowledge of God and with His grace strive to live a good life. Whatever good or truth is found amongst them is looked upon by the Church as a preparation for the Gospel." Second Vatican Council, *Lumen Gentium* (1964), 2.16. Online: http://www.vatican.va/archive/hist_councils/ii_vatican_council/documents/vat-ii_const_19641121_lumen-gentium_en.html [cited 22 April 2014].

25   For a list of scholars that have made overtures toward a thoroughly Jewish Paul, see David J. Rudolph, *A Jew to the Jews: Jewish Contours of Pauline Flexibility in 1 Corinthians 9:19–23* (Tübingen, Germany: Mohr Siebeck, 2011), 211. For a history of the Third Quest along with the important scholars and works that have shaped its assumptions, see N.T. Wright, *Jesus and the Victory of God* (Minneapolis, MN: Fortress, 1996), 83–124.

26   Wright, "The Paul of History and the Apostle of Faith," *Tyndale Bulletin* 29 (1978), 61–88. See also Krister Stendahl, *Paul Among Jews and Gentiles* (London, England: SCM, 1976). Dunn acknowledges his debt to these scholars in *The New Perspective on Paul* (rev. ed.; Grand Rapids, MI: Eerdmans Publishing, 2008), 7.

27   Wright's theology in this area is probably most clearly articulated in *Climax of the Covenant: Christ and the Law in Pauline Theology* (Edinburgh, Scotland: T&T Clark, 1991).

28    Richard Longenecker, *Biblical Exegesis in the Apostolic Period* (Grand Rapids, MI: Eerdmans Publishing, 1999) 77, gives a helpful summary of the idea of corporate solidarity with references for further study.

29    D. Thomas Lancaster, *The Holy Epistle to the Galatians* (Marshfield, MO: First Fruits of Zion, 2011).

30    Zetterholm, *The Formation of Christianity in Antioch*, 128; Fredriksen, *Augustine and the Jews*, 37–38.

31    Rudolph, "Paul's 'Rule in All the Churches' (1 Cor. 7:17–24) and Torah-Defined Ecclesiological Variegation," paper presented at the American Academy of Religion Conference, November 3, 2008.

32    J. Brian Tucker explores the social status of these Gentiles and Paul's struggle to help them understand their identity in this in-between place in *Remain in Your Calling: Paul and the Continuation of Social Identities in 1 Corinthians* (Eugene, OR: Pickwick, 2011).

33    Not just Wright but Albert Schweitzer, Krister Stendahl, and many other scholars over the last century have argued for the prioritization of the "in Christ" identity over personal justification as the center point of Paul's soteriology.

34    This is a major part of Wright's argument in *Justification: God's Plan & Paul's Vision* (Downers Grove, IL: InterVarsity Press, 2009).

35    Tucker, *Remain in Your Calling*. Tucker describes lucidly how Paul took on the role of shaping this identity—Paul was an "entrepreneur" who essentially created a new social category for non-Jewish Christians to inhabit.

36    For more examples and detailed analysis, see Brenda B. Colijn, *Images of Salvation in the New Testament* (Downers Grove, IL: IVP Academic, 2010).

37    This phenomenon is discussed at length in Adam H. Becker and Annette Yoshiko Reed, eds., *The Ways That Never Parted: Jews and Christians in Late Antiquity and the Early Middle Ages* (Minneapolis, MN: Fortress, 2007), as well as by Daniel Boyarin, *Border Lines: The Partition of Judaeo-Christianity* (Philadelphia, PA: University of Pennsylvania, 2004).

38    Randall Price, "Answering the New Covenant Perspective's Charge on the Absence of Restoration to the Land Texts in the New Testament" (paper presented at the Lausanne Consultation on Jewish Evangelism, Chicago, IL, 3 March 2014), 13. "In every case, it is national Israelites taking the Gospel to the Gentiles under the administrative charge of the central apostolic authority in Jerusalem (Acts 15:4)."

39    As defined in Rudolph and Joel Willitts, *Introduction to Messianic Judaism: Its Ecclesial Context and Biblical Foundations* (Grand Rapids, MI: Zondervan, 2013).

40    Many believe that Paul is referring to the church with the term "Israel of God" in Galatians 6:16. However, this is not necessarily or even likely the case. See Peter Richardson, *Israel in the Apostolic Church* (Cambridge, MA: Cambridge University Press, 1969), 74–84 for an in-depth discussion of this verse.

41    The perceived necessity of this theological shift to ensure the church's survival is discussed in Zetterholm, *The Formation of Christianity in Antioch*.

42    Kinzer, *Postmissionary Messianic Judaism*, 15–16.

43    *Pirkei Avot* 1.12.

44    Attributed to the French writer Honoré de Balzac, though his original statement did not carry the same meaning, and the quote has evolved over time: "Le secret des grandes fortunes sans cause apparente est un crime oublié, parce qu'il a été proprement fait."

45    See Rashi's commentary on Exodus 22.

46    For a more in-depth discussion of an ethical Messianic Jewish stance on the Israeli-Palestinian conflict, see Russ Resnik, "An Ethical Window: Framing a Messianic Jewish Moral Perspective," paper presented at the Hashivenu Forum, 2013.

47    D.T. Lancaster, *Torah Club: Chronicles of the Messiah* (Marshfield, MO: First Fruits of Zion, 2014), bound edition, 1402–3.

48    See again Rudolph and Willits, *Introduction to Messianic Judaism*, for help in identifying Messianic Jewish synagogues that are theologically balanced and ecclesiologically mature enough to be of help here.

49    Lancaster discusses this phenomenon in *The Holy Epistle to the Galatians*, 188–91.

50    James D.G. Dunn, in *The Acts of the Apostles* (Peterborough: Epworth, 1996), 285, prefers to use different terminology—"flexibility and adaptability"—in order to absolve Paul of outright deception. However, the fact remains that if Paul seriously differed from the other apostles, we are in a quandary.

51    Troy W. Martin, "The Covenant of Circumcision (Genesis 17:9–14) and the Situational Antitheses in Galatians 3:28," *JBL* 122:1 (2003): 111–25.

52    Rudolph, "Paul's 'Rule in All the Churches,'" 7.

53    See Tucker, *Remain in Your Calling*.

54    Messianic Jew Theophilus Lucky recorded and strongly condemned these practices in *The Peculiar People* 11.1 (1889). Online: http://vineofdavid.org/_php/download.php?file=The_Peculiar_People_1889_Lucky.pdf [cited 9 April 2014].

55    The consummate work on this subject is Kinzer, *Postmissionary Messianic Judaism*.

56 See Rudolph, *A Jew to the Jews*, 74; Kinzer, *Postmissionary Messianic Judaism*, 72–73.

57 Johannes Munck, *Christ and Israel: An Interpretation of Romans 9–11* (trans. Ingeborg Nixon; Philadelphia, PA: Fortress, 1967), 136.

58 For a more thorough explanation of this passage, see Mark Kinzer, "Final Destinies: Qualifications for Receiving an Eschatological Inheritance" (paper presented at the Borough Park Symposium, New York, October 2007), 5.

59 Philip A. Cunningham and Didier Pollefeyt, "The Triune One, the Incarnate Logos, and Israel's Covenantal Life" in *Christ Jesus and the Jewish People Today: New Explorations of Theological Interrelationships* (eds. Philip A. Cunningham, Joseph Sievers, Mary C. Boys, Hans Hermann Henrix, and Jesper Svartvik; Grand Rapids, MI: Eerdmans Publishing, 2011), 183–201.

60 For a multifaceted exploration of this idea, see the collected essays in Philip A. Cunningham et al., eds., *Christ Jesus and the Jewish People Today: New Explorations of Theological Interrelationships* (Grand Rapids, MI: Eerdmans Publishing, 2011).

61 For a recent example see Price, "Answering the New Covenant Perspective's Charge."

62 John Ronning, *The Jewish Targums and John's Logos Theology* (Grand Rapids, MI: Baker, 2010), 180. Cited in *Chronicles of the Messiah*, 243–45.

63 Lancaster, *Chronicles of the Messiah*, 236.

64 See also Kinzer, "Final Destinies," 24–25.

# About the Author

Jacob Fronczak has spent the past fifteen years ministering in local churches in numerous support and leadership roles. He completed his M.Div. through Liberty University in 2013 and is currently the lead pastor at Eastpoint Community Church in Coldwater, Michigan.

A member of First Fruits of Zion's creative team, Jacob is also a vocal supporter of the modern-day Messianic Jewish renewal, and has contributed to Messianic dialogue through contributions to *Messiah Journal* and *Kesher*. He believes Messianic Judaism has a critical role in connecting twenty-first-century Christianity with its first-century Jewish roots.